Cyrillize it! Кириллизируй!

Cyrillize it!

A guide on Cyrillic typography for graphic designers

Yana Vekshyna

Кириллизируй!

Яна Векшина

Гид по кириллической типографике для графических дизайнеров

niggli

Contents

Letters

Interview

Variations

Epilogue

References

Meet the letters

There is a difference in the way we pronounce the letters of the alphabet, and the sounds they actually represent. The following table provides the approximate English phonetic equivalents of each letter of the Russian alphabet. Ukrainian and Belarusian alphabets include several different characters, but generally share the same letterforms with Russian.

Аа A as in "f<u>a</u>ther"	**Бб** B as in "<u>b</u>ad"	**Вв** V as in "<u>v</u>ine"	**Гг** G as in "<u>g</u>ood"	**Дд** D as in "<u>d</u>o"
Ее YE as in "<u>ye</u>s"	**Ёё** YO as in "<u>yo</u>ur"	**Жж** ZH as in "plea<u>s</u>ure"	**Зз** Z as in "<u>z</u>oo"	**Ии** I as in "pol<u>i</u>ce"
Йй Y as in "to<u>y</u>"	**Кк** K as in "<u>k</u>ept"	**Лл** L as in "<u>l</u>ine"	**Мм** M as in "<u>m</u>ap"	**Нн** N as in "<u>n</u>ot"
Оо O as in "m<u>o</u>re"	**Пп** P as in "<u>p</u>et"	**Рр** rolled R	**Сс** S as in "<u>s</u>et"	**Тт** T as in "<u>t</u>op"
Уу U as in "t<u>oo</u>l"	**Фф** F as in "<u>f</u>ace"	**Хх** H as in "<u>h</u>ole"	**Цц** TS as in "<u>ts</u>ar"	**Чч** CH as in "<u>ch</u>eck"
Шш SH as in "<u>sh</u>arp"	**Щщ** SHCH as in "fre<u>sh ch</u>eese"	**Ъъ** hard sign	**Ыы** IH as in "<u>i</u>ll"	**Ьь** soft sign
Ээ E as in "m<u>e</u>t"	**Юю** YU as in "<u>u</u>se"	**Яя** YA as in "<u>ya</u>rd"		

Introduction

Введение

It is not a secret that we live in a world where constant interaction between cultures strongly influences our everyday life. We meet people, get exposed to products, hear the news about countries that we didn't even suspect existed several years ago. Our cultural landscapes are expanding and becoming more diverse thanks to the development of digital media.

For visual communicators, language and more specifically, type, is essential and one of the most powerful tools for conveying messages and creating meaning. And the more tools you can master, the more powerful you become. Simple as that.

The fear of the unknown can be a great obstacle when it comes to working with other scripts. Different origins and forms of script, and the inability to read the characters generate insecurity among designers. But however complex it looks, it is important to remember that script is a system. And like any system it can be explored, analysed and explained. Human writing habits still have a lot in common regardless of the country. Different script systems have also been influencing each other for centuries. And the evolution of script into digital format has also created a lot of limitations, that in this case are beneficial for designers in a sense of making the type easier to work with.

Current design practices also show that proficiency in foreign languages is not particularly necessary in order to work with foreign script systems. Studying and learning the distinctive typographic rules and type structure characteristics of the script prove to be an adequate base for creating successful multi-scriptual design projects.

For decades Latin script has been a dominant type system and a great influence in the world of graphic design, due to its rich history and progressive development. It has been setting an example to other script systems in terms of the evolution of printing type. However, while foreign designers often obtain the knowledge of both their native and Latin types by default, in the Western world getting a chance to learn foreign scripts is still a rare opportunity. There are only a few higher education institutions that provide such practices, and mostly for type designers.

It is important to understand that each script has its own special features, that are essential to know in order to create a legible design. However close by the origin, it would still be a mistake to work with any type according to Latin rules. Each script requires different typographic settings, such as leading, tracking, size of the characters etc. It is also important to be able to identify the good quality typefaces, which needs a little bit of type design expertise.

So now the time has come to dive into the world of Cyrillic type, with its rules, peculiarities and turbulent history. Although foreign scripts might look somewhat intimidating at first, in the case of Cyrillic we are lucky, since it closely resembles Latin script in terms of origin, development and typographic rules. To put it short: Latin graphics are the foundation of modern Cyrillic type.

Like Latin, Cyrillic is a script written from left to right. Characters in both types share basic common features, such as hight, width, contrasts, angles of bowls, serifs, stems, strokes. 16 uppercase and 12 lowercase characters in modern Cyrillic fonts have identical letterforms in Latin.

Today the Cyrillic alphabet is used by more than 250 million people in the world. The largest number of users stem from Russia, Ukraine and Bulgaria, followed by Belarus, Serbia and many more Slavic and non-Slavic countries. When Bulgaria entered the European Union in 2007, Cyrillic became the third official script of the European Union, after Latin and Greek scripts. It is also the second most used content language on the internet after English [1]. The extended Cyrillic alphabet is used by more than 100 languages and includes more than 145 letters [2].

The Cyrillic alphabet was invented specifically for Slavic languages and special sounds. A single letter represents a single sound, which makes the reading process fairly easy. Each word is pronounced the way it is written, unlike for example in French or English where a combination of several letters may produce different sounds. For a foreigner, it would be enough to learn the sound that each letter represents, in order to be able to read straight away.

[1] Data of 2021, by W3Techs
[2] Unicode version 10.0

While Latin-based languages use diacritics to represent special regional sounds, in Cyrillic the characters often tend to change their letterform rather than acquire a diacritical element [1].

Кк Ӄӄ Ҝҝ Ҡҡ Ҟҟ Ӈӈ
Ее Ёё Ӗӗ Єє Ҫҫ Єє

[1] [1] Letterform variations of Cyrillic letters K and E in different languages

Cyrillic type as we know it today is still in development. In the 18th century it went through a drastic redesign executed by a person, who was neither a type designer nor had any knowledge of the field. In addition to this, decades of stagnation in type design during the Soviet times have resulted in a 300 year quest for harmony and a unified construction system of all characters, which still continues today. Due to its bumpy history, Cyrillic type design is still a fairly new practice in Eastern European countries. However in the last ten years the industry has made a strong push towards the revival of Cyrillic type and graphic design. This has encouraged the emergence of new type foundries, the formation of a relevant professional community, and cooperation with Western designers.

In this book we will mainly focus on the exploration of Russian alphabet and its 33 letters in particular, since it's the most used one. Additionally, we will address the alternative forms presented in Bulgarian and Serbian alphabets and their correlation with Latin script, and speculate on the future of Cyrillic script and its relevance in the world of design.

Relevance Актуальность

Cyrillic is the new black

In the last 15 years Cyrillic type has become more visible in Western countries. After the collapse of the Soviet Union and the fall of the Iron Curtain, which separated the Eastern block from the developing West, a new generation of artists and designers was given an opportunity to join the world arena and demonstrate their talent. And fashion probably played a major role in this process. Emerging Eastern European fashion brands, such as Gosha Rubchinsky, Vatements, Andrey Artyomov [3–6, next page] made major breakthroughs across runways in Paris, London and New York, proudly flashing Cyrillic slogans and a trashy style of the underprivileged soviet working class. In the design world, the interest was sparked by several publications dedicated to Eastern European culture, for example "CCCP. Cosmic Communist Constructions Photographed" by Taschen or "Russian Criminal Tattoo Encyclopaedia" by Fuel [2].

[2] First volume of "Russian Criminal Tattoo Encyclopaedia" published by Fuel in 2004

 For foreigners, Cyrillic letters looked mysterious and exotic, similar to a trend in Japanese kanji tattoos earlier. Lately the tables have actually turned: more and more clothes and tattoos with Cyrillic can be seen on the streets of Japan, South Korea and China. Some foreign brands have picked up the trend and also produce clothing collections with alien looking characters. Young people quickly took on a style that represented the crazy, adventurous and controversial life of the post-Soviet 90s – an association with exciting, exotic, trashy youth that they never had. This way Cyrillic quickly found its way into the underground world, and from there was adopted by musicians and designers in search for a rough and unpolished expression.

 The social and political situation of the last two decades in Eastern Europe has also greatly influenced the popularisation of the script. Before then no one had any idea what was going on in that part of the world, but in the last 25 years Eastern European countries through

Cyrillic letters — f
heavy — are not lo
but for being differ
even slightly intim

[3] Campaign for 2015 collection of Ukrainian
designer Yulia Yefimtchuk

[4] Collaboration of Russian designer Gosha
Rubchinskiy with Adidas

t, angular and
d for their beauty,
nt, alienating and
ating. Anastasiia Fedorova, writer

[5] Socks by Russian brand
Sputnik 1985

[6] "Style" turtleneck
by American designer
Heron Preston

several loud political statements, revolutions, wars, have turned peoples' heads in their direction. The world was given the chance to finally observe and rethink the image of post-soviet countries, thus creating the concept of the "new east", which was quickly appropriated by pop-culture. Although this "new east" is rather a myth and collection of stereotypes and attributes, than a true depiction of post-Soviet life [1].

Nevertheless, Cyrillic started spreading, and the lack of knowledge about it became apparent. One of the biggest issues with the script still today is that very few typefaces include the Cyrillic family. When planning a project with Cyrillic, be prepared to face serious limitations with the choice of typefaces. In most cases, fonts developed in Western countries don't include Cyrillic at all. And those which do, however, sometimes make clear mistakes in the characters, making the typeface a bad choice for graphic designers in the sense of readability, balance and aesthetic impression. Even type design giants have typefaces in their collection that have pretty contentious issues with the Cyrillic part [7]. This mostly seems to happen when type foundries trust non-native designers to develop the font without consulting the specialists from Eastern European countries, which was especially common during the Soviet times.

[1] "Word up: how Cyrillic typography became the lingua franca for underground fashion", Anastasia Fedorova, The Calvert Journal, June 6, 2014

ФЕОДАЛКА

[7]
Arial, Regular

Φ is too short, E is too wide, Д, Л and K are too narrow; left stroke of Л is too straight and should be more tilted to the right - it's an outdated way of designing this letter

блюдечко

Open Sans, Regular

The tail of б is too long and stretching too far to the right; the left strokes of л and д are too tilted, the angle should be smaller; descenders of д are too long and left stroke is connected too close to the edge; the arch of ч is too curvy, probably repeating the arches of Latin characters

лавджой

Times New Roman, Regular

The left stroke of л should be tilted like in д; the middle line of ж lies too high and the upper legs with drop elements are spreading too wide making the upper part of the letter too massive; the breve above й is spreading too wide and should have the same drop elements as other characters of the typeface

2 "Font scandal at
FIFA World Cup",
type.today,
July 10, 2018

In 2014 there was a big typographic scandal at FIFA World Cup Russia [2]. The Portuguese brand agency Brandia Central presented the identity for the championship, accompanied by the typeface "Dusha" that was developed specifically for the cause. It was supposed to be based on Russian traditional historic letterforms and compliment the rounded logo. According to the claims of the type designer, who was hired to produce the functional font, he was given drawings of the characters created by the studio's Russian intern and was forbidden to make any changes. As a result, the world saw a typeface with unnaturally distorted characters in both Latin and Cyrillic sets. On top of that, the obviously decorative type that was intended for limited use in headlines and titles, was misused in big text settings [8].

[8] Official type-
face of 2018 FIFA
World Championship
"Dusha" with high-
lights on question-
able details from
type.today editors

ABCDEFGHIJKLMN
OPQRSTUVWXYZ

АБВГДЕЖЗИЙКЛ
МНОПРСТУФХЦЧ
ШЩЪЫЬЭЮЯ

It doesn't mean however, that Western type foundries and designers can't be trusted. Although, it is always a good idea to consult a native user of the script when working on a project that contains Cyrillic type. Typotheque (Netherlands), Production Type (France and China), Commercial Type (USA, UK) are companies that have a large number of Cyrillic fonts developed by Russian type designers. Black Foundry (France) and Pangram Pangram (Canada) are also considered to be one of the best Western studios producing Cyrillic. With both studios counting type designers from Eastern Europe in their teams. Grilli Type (Switzerland) has also recently hired consultants and is remodelling the Cyrillic versions of their typefaces. And let's not forget the growing number of Eastern European type foundries, producing more and more fresh, experimental, good quality fonts. Particularly notable are Paratype, Brownfox, Letterhead, Contrast Foundry, CSTM Fonts, AlfaBravo, Ivan Tsanko Type, Fontfabric and many more.

Although typographic rules for Cyrillic are not extremely different from Latin, misuse also occurs in the graphic design field. A common trick, which foreign designers try to pull off, is using Cyrillic letters as a quirky substitute for Latin. This notion is called "faux Cyrillic" and can be traced all the way back to the times of the Cold War, when the United States was using this propaganda tool for the dehumanization of their Soviet enemy [3]. My favourite example is a shirt designed by H&M with the meaningless set of characters НЦМДИТУ ЦЙІТ3D [9]. Since native speakers read their letters automatically, for any native Cyrillic user this would look like random letters accidentally typed on keyboard, despite the H&M designers actually intending to write HUMANITY UNITED. Tricks like this tend to look more like cultural appropriation than good design. A more elegant solution would be writing the phrase in Cyrillic transliteration [10]. Since each Cyrillic character represents one sound, it is quite easy to transliterate any word from any language based on its spelling. This method is quite trendy at the moment, and might give your design a stylish humorous feel to it.

[3] "The trouble with Яussиаи. The West's reprehensible misuse of Cyrillic continues", Kevin Rothrock, Medusa, September 21, 2017

[9] H&M hoodie with a gibberish slogan

[10] Sputnik1985 t-shirt saying "I don't like you" in Cyrillic transliteration

[9]   [10]

Of course, graphic design projects with Cyrillic are more common in the countries of native users. Nevertheless, there are quite a few successful projects, realised by Western designers and design studios. And hopefully with the popularisation of knowledge about other script systems, there will be more to come.

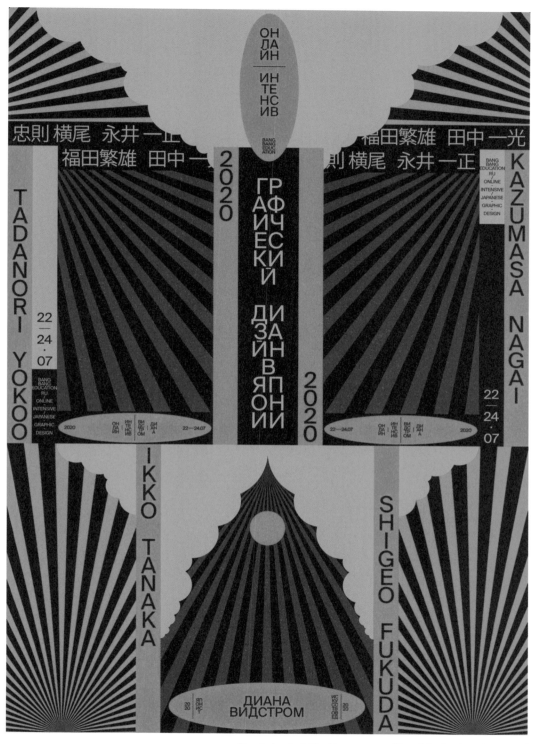

Electric Red Studio, poster "Graphic Design in Japan"
for Bang Bang Education School, 2020

Strelka
15.07 / 23:00
Пика — Пика
Palmistry
www.strelka.com
(UK, live)
Throwing
Shade
(UK, Dj Set)

14, bldg 5a, Bersenevskaya embankment

#strelkasummer
2016

Anna Kulachek, Palmistry and Throwing Shade
at Strelka poster, 2016

Rem Koolhaas
Рем Колхас
18:30–19:00

Benjamin Bratton
Бенджамин Браттон
18:30 - 19:00

Shifting social norms and emerging technologies ch
the future of our cities — at the Strelka New Normal s

НОВАЯ НОРМ
ШОУКЕЙС
03—04.07.20

Anna Kulachek, Strelka's The N

ster, 2017

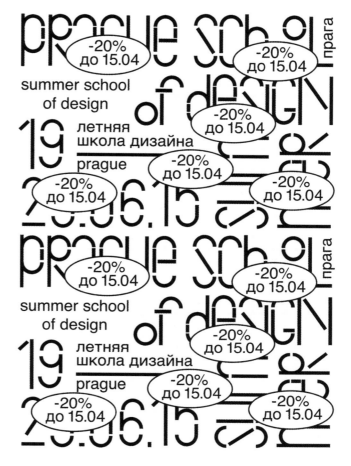

Anna Kulachek, identity for the Summer Prague
School of Design, 2015

Anna Kulachek,
Summer Closing Party
Invitation, Strelka, 2017

Dmitry Kavka, poster for New Year's market, 2008

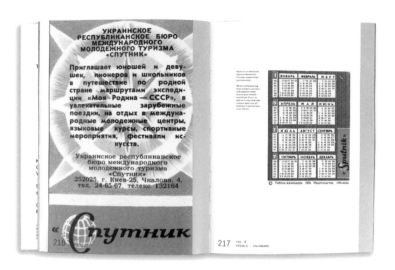

Sebastian Schubmehl,
book "Kyiv Type: Graphic
Design & Typography – Visual
Treasures from Kyiv", 2020

Anatoly Grashchenko, visual identity for a retrospective experimental
music festival of the work of Alvin Lucier, 2017

U,N,A collective,
book "Znak. Ukrainian
Trademarks 1960–80s", 2019

Anatoly Grashchenko, visual identity for a retrospective
experimental music festival of the work of Alvin Lucier, 2017

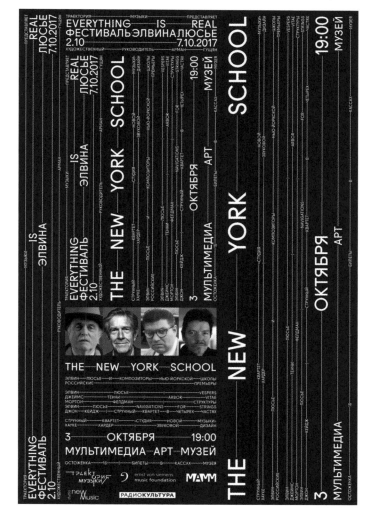

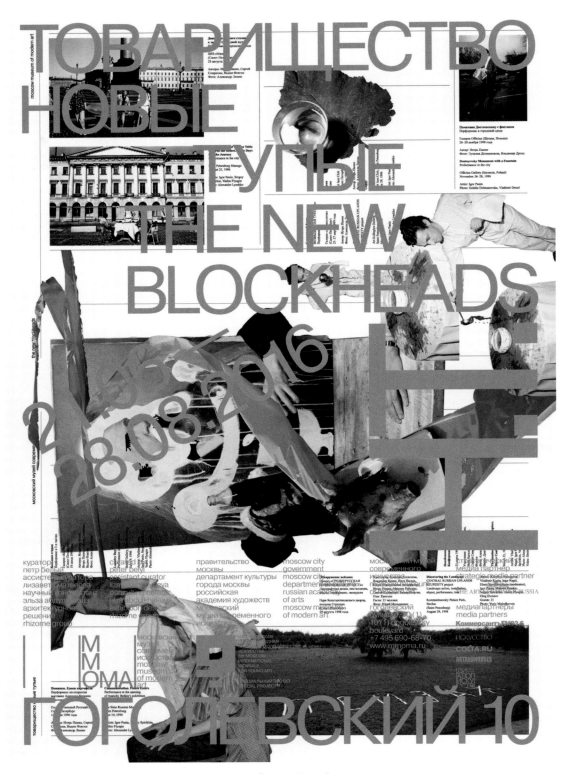

Roman Gornitsky, poster for the exhibition of "Новые Тупые"
art group in Moscow Museum of Modern Art, 2016

ТОВАРИЩЕСТВО НОВЫЕ ТУПЫЕ

THE NEW BLOCKHEADS

21.06–28.08.2016

ГОГОЛЕВСКИЙ 10

Roman Gornitsky, poster for the exhibition of "Новые Тупые"
art group in Moscow Museum of Modern Art, 2016

СКУЛЬПТУРА
ИЗ ПРИРОДНЫХ
МАТЕРИАЛОВ
LAND ART
SCULPTURE

MASTERCLASS

06.12
08.12
16:00

LEADING
LISA
CHUHLANTSEVA

300₽
ГАЛЕРЕЯ «НА ШАБОЛОВКЕ»
М. ШАБОЛОВСКАЯ, М. ТУЛЬСКАЯ,
СЕРПУХОВСКИЙ ВАЛ, 24/2
ЧАСЫ РАБОТЫ: ВТ–ВС, 11:00–20:00
КОНТАКТЫ: +7 (495) 954 30 09
INFO-NASHABOLOVKE@VZMOSCOW.RU
VK: VZNASHABOLOVKE
FB / INST: NASHABOLOVKE.GALLERY
WWW.NASHABOLOVKE-GALLERY.COM

6+

Anastasia Zhurba (Groza Design), poster for a master class about land art sculpture, 2017

Anna-Maria Kandales-Vorobeva (Groza Design), poster for generative experimental art exhibition, 2016

Alexander Vasin (Groza Design),
CD cover design "Vladimir Spivakov.
Russian Music Masterpieces", 2020

Electric Red Studio and Strelka Institute, poster for
a research project "The Terraforming", 2019

Aliona Solomadina, visual identity for the
project "Poetry and Performance", 2021

Artem Tataurov,
contemporary vyaz
stylization, 2018

TRY
ND
ICE

Artem Latyshev, poster for music festival "Cage. Our Spring Will Come", 2021

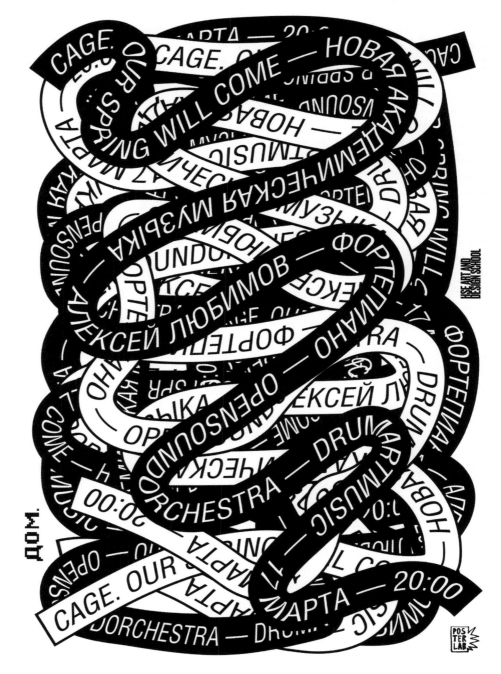

Peter Bankov, poster for the exhibition "The New State of the Living", 2019

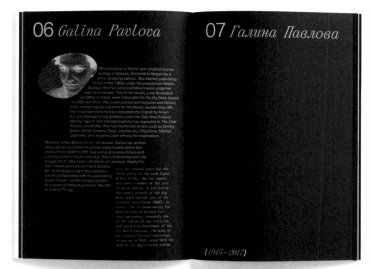

Yana Vekshyna, book design for a poetry collection
"Turbulent Days" by Galina Pavlova, 2021

Peter Bankov, poster for the educational
project "How to weigh words", 2016

Peter Bankov, poster for Europenian School
of Design workshop in Frankfurt, 2018

Alexandr Kuznetsov, a series of self-promotional
posters "Workoholism/W.H.N.S./Posters 19", 2019

Alexandr Kuznetsov, a seri
"Spirit vs.Spirit/H.N.S./F

Facultative Works, cover
for the single "The Knight"
by Naadya, 2021

Alexandr Kuznetsov, a series of self-promotional posters
"Spirit vs.Spirit / H.N.S. / Posters 21", 2021

Artem Tataurov,
"Monument" lettering,
vyaz stylization, 2018

Interview Интервью

Anna Kulachek

Anna is a Ukrainian graphic designer currently working and living in New York. Besides other creative projects, she works as an art-director for the Moscow Media, Architecture and Design institute "Strelka", which is known for its expressive, colourful bi-lingual brand identity. Winner of multiple design awards, she also teaches aspiring designers in several Russian educational institutions.

In one of your older interviews you said that one of your big passions is fashion. One of the names that you mentioned was Gosha Rubchinskiy, who uses a lot of Cyrillic typography in his clothes. Why do you think Cyrillic became so trendy at some point?

At some point different languages like Japanese, Chinese, then Russian were trendy. I think the new generation has grown up, they stopped feeling shy, stopped using Latin and pretending to be American or European. Gosha Rubchinskiy was one of the first, who made a statement: "That's who I am." When something happens sincerely and honestly, it attracts attention, since it's something unique. After the collapse of the Soviet Union everyone was ashamed of it, everyone wanted to live like in Europe. Gosha showed the aesthetics of our uptown neighbourhoods to the world and the world got hooked. I think it's more of a spirit. Our weird characters, trashy unadorned reality opposed to unrealistic Dior fashion, for example.

We live in the times of globalism. Everything gets mixed. Before different design schools and movements existed. There was Japanese, Polish, and Dutch design. Now if you look at any graphic design blog, you won't be able to guess where the designer is from. Whether he's Swiss, Russian or American. The internet has granted us a very quick exchange of information.

For me, the most in typography is prop with three fonts m

You live and work abroad, and probably collaborate with Western designers. Are there any trends regarding Cyrillic type happening at the moment?

Western designers are very curious about Cyrillic. I took part in several projects, where I was asked to use two different scripts. In my opinion, the combination of different scripts creates interesting textures. That's why I like working with Strelka's bi-lingual design, using both English and Russian. Sometimes working only with Latin feels more boring to me than mixing several scripts. Cyrillic is rarely seen in the West and when you add it to the usual Latin, it looks like a special product. Americans don't understand and don't use it in their projects, that's why they get excited when they see me working with it.

My friend Maria Doreuli [1] is often hired for developing Cyrillic families for the fonts, because most American designers have no clue how to design it. The 2018 FIFA World Championship hired foreign designers to develop a typeface for them and I couldn't look at those letters, they looked absolutely horrible. However, for them, maybe, it seemed interesting. And if I didn't know Russian I might have had another opinion. There is a possibility that without our traditional education, Western type designers can find new ways of designing Cyrillic.

Since you combine Latin and Cyrillic in your projects a lot, can you explain what the major differences between these two scripts are?

There is a huge difference. First of all, there still aren't enough Cyrillic typefaces. More than 10 years ago, but still not enough. We have very few well designed sans-serif fonts. Perhaps this is due to the lack of Cyrillic type designers. Roughly speaking, in the West every second person designs typefaces, and we only have Maria and five more good type designers. They don't have enough time to satisfy the

[1] Find the interview with Maria Doreuli on page 115

ortant thing in rtion. I can work entire life.

[2] Lazurski was de-
signed by Paratype
in 1984. Inspired
by 16th century
typefaces of Ital-
ian Renaissance

[3] Fugue is a geo-
metric sans-serif
typeface designed
by Radim Peško

demand. Second of all, as we all know, the modern Cyrillic type was created mechanically by Peter the Great, and sometimes it's harder to create balanced lines of texts compared to Latin. Before everyone considered this a disadvantage, but lately it bothers me less and less. Good quality typefaces make any text look great. For instance, I am working a lot with Lazurski font [2]. Although it's an old style typeface, it never goes out of fashion and guarantees beautiful timeless results. I adore it!

A whole other issue is finding a typeface that would look good both in English and Russian. In Strelka's design we use Fugue font [3]. It looks very balanced in both languages, thus I have forgotten about this issue for a while. But generally it's a big problem.

To be honest, I'm quite superficial about type. I never search for the latest novelties in type design. For me, the most important thing in typography is proportion. I can work with three fonts my entire life. Because I form all my designs with the help of imagery, colours and shapes.

Why is it important for a foreign graphic designer to have the ability to identify and use good quality typefaces in their projects?

When you work with a client you want what's best for them. It's the aesthetics of such an approach and professional responsibility. You sell a client something he has no clue about, and it's important to be honest and give your best.

Of course, as a concept, you can consciously pick a bad type-face for your design. A couple of times when I worked on party posters I was searching for typefaces on Dafont and found some "pure dia-monds" there. Trash design is also a thing. But for serious projects it's important to use good quality materials, since it has to be legible. I do respect the type designers' craft.

From your perspective, what do graphic designers need to know in order to start working with Cyrillic?

Cyrillic and Latin are quite similar. Thus knowing the rules of Latin typography is already sufficient. First, I would set Cyrillic the same way as Latin and find someone to consult with regarding the hyphenation, hanging prepositions and so on. It's hard to grasp all of it, you have to grow up with the language, feel it.

I've also been noticing that Cyrillic doesn't always look good in big size, especially next to Latin. Sometimes it has a lot of "holes". So I'm trying to perceive the text as a texture and adjust things manually. With the growing number of well designed Cyrillic typefaces we are moving closer and closer to Latin quality.

Currently there are no tendencies of teaching foreign script systems in international educational institutions. Do you think it could be a beneficial initiative? Or should everyone just stick to their thing and keep consulting each other?

I find it very interesting, to have an opportunity to learn about Chinese or Arabic, for example. At least the basics. I have a friend who is currently working on a bi-lingual website for Hong Kong, and he's facing a lot of troubles with type sizing, proportions etc. If he had the basic knowledge of Chinese script, it would have saved him a lot of time and stress. Nevertheless, I would have ordered the development of Cyrillic typeface from a native designer. That's just me [laughs].

Regarding your work for "Strelka" institute. Why was the brand identity developed by a London-based studio OK-RM, not someone local?

It all happened before I started working there. As far as I know, first, there were attempts at development by Russian designers, but then the institute took a more globalised approach – inviting international speakers, organising programs in English – and decided to consult a Western studio. In my opinion, it's also our Russian thing, to invite foreigners, let them build something to set an example. Still they were consulted by Ukrainian designer Misha Smetana, who supervised the Cyrillic part, since a bi-lingual approach was very important.

In 2014 Strelka invited me to develop the identity further. The institute started expanding and a simple grid offered by OK-RM wasn't enough anymore. I began to play around, adding shapes and colours. We used the original identity as a soil to grow a more playful and flexible approach. Strelka keeps asking me to change it every year and I say: "Why? It's perfect!". Considering that ironically OK-RM has picked my favourite Lazurski as one of the identity fonts.

By the way, a little funny story about Lazurski to wrap up the interview. I used it in a project for an American music institution, and they have asked me about the font. I told them about a Russian designer Vadim Lazurski and it completely freaked them out. For some reason Americans could not comprehend the use of a Russian font.

In the Cyrillic, you
intentional form-m
bination of elemen
a deep understand
structure, with a ve
of adaptation to hi

В кириллице соед
ёмы искусственн
вания знаков нар
рукописного поче
глубокого поним
этой письменнос

ave a degree of
king, and a com-
that require
g of the script
specific history
orical models.

Gerry Leonidas, typographer

няются при-
о формообразо-
ду с традициями
ка, что требует
ия эволюции
I.

Джерри Леонидас, типограф

His
tory
Исто
рия

How it all began

[1] Phonemic struc-
ture means the
transfer of the
sound of words by
written and some
notional characters

Cyrillic is a phonetic writing system that was developed in the 9th–10th centuries in the First Bulgarian Empire. Graphically the basis of the script takes origins in Eastern Greek uncial script [11], but phonemic [1] structure was inherited from earlier Glagolitic [12].

[11] Codex Tischendorfianus IV, 10th century, an example of Greek uncial script that served as an inspiration for Cyrillic alphabet

[12] Kiev Missal, second half of the 10th century, one of the oldest samples of Glagolitic writing

For a long time it was believed that Cyrillic was the oldest Slavic alphabet, however after the discovery of 11th century religious miscellany Glagolita Clozianus in 1836 and further manuscripts and inscriptions written in Glagolitic, historians have introduced a new theory about the primacy of Glagolitic over Cyrillic [2]. Still early specimens of Glagolitic are very rare and hard to date.

As in many other cases of language and script development, religion and politics have played the major role in the development of Cyrillic. In the 9th century the power conflict over the Slavic lands between Byzantine Empire and King Louis the German has led to the invention of the first Slavic script and translation of biblical scholarship into Slavic languages. This has also contributed to the education of common Slavic people and the development of literary language. The most important development stages of Cyrillic script system are:

1.

Invention of Glagolitic alphabet by Christian missionaries Cyril (this is where the name "Cyrillic" comes from) and Methodius in 863 CE in Great Moravia [3]. The alphabet didn't gain a lot of popularity because of its complexity.

2.

Development of early Cyrillic alphabet by the pupils of Cyril and Methodius in 893 CE in the First Bulgarian Empire. This time the alphabet was redesigned and developed based mostly on the Greek letterforms, some characters were taken from Hebrew and Latin. However it still kept the phonemic system of Glagolitic because of the sounds in Slavic languages, which could not be represented by other alphabets. The theories regarding the origins and authors of both alphabets are still being debated today because of the very few historic artefacts.

3.

Reformation and "latinisation" of Cyrillic by the Russian Emperor Peter the Great in 1708-1710. Peter was obsessed with an idea of bringing the Russian Empire closer to progressive European culture and politics. These reforms affected the alphabet too. Letters were redesigned to look more like Latin, but this was done in such an amateur way, that Cyrillic only reached its standard letterforms in the 19th century, hundreds of years after the development of high standards of Western type.

4.

Repressive type reforms of the Soviet government in 1917-91 that led to the destruction of a big part of typographic historical heritage and slowed the industry down for a century. These limitations, however, have led to the rise of hand-written type and lettering, and the development of the distinguishing graphical language of the Soviet Constructivism.

4 Uncial is a script
written entirely
in capital letters,
commonly used in
4th-8th centuries
by Latin and Greek
scribes

When it comes to the graphical styles of Cyrillic script, its earliest graphical version was called *ustav.* Ustav is an uncial [4] style of writing that was characterised by having vertically straight characters with only one weight and height. Letters were not connected and had equal distances between them, there was no separation into words. The text was very thoroughly written, reminding a printed type. Graphically ustav was strongly inspired by the Greek majuscule script [13].

НИЖАЄГО҇ТНЖЄННОТ҇
КРⸯ҃ВН·ННОТⷹПО
ХОТНПЛⷺТЬСКꙐ
А·ННОТⷹПОХОТН
МЖ҃ЬⷧСКꙐ·НⷹОТⷹ
Б҃ⷬАРОДНШАСⷯНСЛО

МⷹНⷺ·ПРⷺⷣДⷹМⷹ
НОЇⷤ БⸯꙐⷭ·ꙖКО
ПⸯРⷺⷡⸯНЇМЄНЄБⷺⷱ
НОТⷹНСПⷧ҃НЄНН
ꙖКГО·МⷹІВⷧСН
ПРⷩꙖ҃ХОМⷹ БЛАГО

5 Chekunova A. Русское кириллическое письмо XI-XVIII вв. Moscow: RGGU, 2010

[13] Ostromir Gospels, 1056-57 CE, the oldest dated Eastern Slavic manuscript - example of ustav

Gradually by the 15th century ustav transformed into *poluustav* (semi-uncial). This style of writing could be written faster, and already contained ligatures, diacritical characters and more varieties of letter-forms [14]. In the middle of the 16th century the first Eastern Slavonic printing was founded and since then poluustav was used as a main printing type and didn't change much until Peter's reforms[5].

Ивыидеиѡлегъ набрегъ · ивоѣватинача́ мно́ гоѹ
вннства сотвори · ѡколограⷣа грикомъбиразбиша
многыполаты́ · ипо ркгошаⷰ цр҃ кви · ануⷲе́ има
хоу пⷧⷮѣнникы · ѡпⷮѣха посикаху́ дроугн́ аⷤⷥⷷⷨ
тахоу · иныи́ ѭ ераⷭⷮрила хоу · адроугы́ н
вморⷷⷡⷷ метахоу · ииⷩⷷа многатворⷷа хоу роусь
грикомъ...Єлико жератпнии творⷯⷮѣ ти :

[14] "The Tale of Bygone Years" from the Radziwill Chronicle, 15th century - example of poluustav

Ustav and poluustav were formal and complicated scripts for common people and were used mostly for the purpose of the church. This is why in the second half of the 14th century *skoropis* (meaning "fast writing") started to develop. The script looked very dynamic, letters were written in one nib movement and connected with each other. Therefore it could be written much faster than poluustav and had an even bigger variety of letterforms, which is why it was mostly used in more practical everyday needs [15]. It was also the only kind of Cyrillic type that developed naturally, based on real handwriting and nib traces, just like Latin. In some modern italic letterforms the influence of skoropis can still be found.

And one more important type style worth talking about is *vyaz*. It is a decorative type that appeared at the end of the 14th century and was in a way similar to Blackletter style in Latin. Vyaz is characterised by interesting ligatures and different character sizes, which may vary for the sake of overall composition. It is still used for creating a historic Slavic style [16].

[16] Example of vyaz from the Illustrated Chronicle of Ivan the Terrible, 1568-76 CE

And then, in the 18th century came Peter the Great ...

Peter the Great

Peter I, undoubtedly one of the most influential rulers of the Russian Empire, who reigned 1682–1725, had a dream to "cut a door to Europe" [1]. He was greatly inspired by Western Europe and the Enlightenment, and implemented a set of reforms that led to cultural, political and scientific revolutions. Type was one of them.

[1] Phrase from the poem "The Bronze Horseman" by A. Pushkin, 1837

Analysis of the new type developed by Peter indicates that the emperor might have been inspired by King Louis XIV of France, who was also carrying out type reforms [2]. In 1692 the Sun King commissioned the design of a new typeface for the use of the Royal Print Office. As a result, a special typeface called "Romain du Roi" [17] was developed by typographer Jacques Jaugeon and punch cutter Philippe Grandjean of the special Bignon Commission. The first book that was printed with this typeface was found in the library of Peter, and might have served as inspiration. But while for King Louis this affair was just a development of a new typeface, that was another variation of Antiqua, Peter had a grand plan of reforming the whole script.

[2] Lecture "Cyrillic and Latin: yesterday and today" by Vladimir Yefimov, Moscow, 2010

There was no pre-existing natural script basis for the development of a new type. But Peter was so obsessed with the idea of making Russia a European country, that no one had the power or will to resist the king's desire to reform the type. Thus the reform ended up being artificial and forced.

Historians assume that there were several parties involved in the development process of the new type. First the Emperor himself created the primary sketches. Then military engineer and draftsman Kuhlenbach refined and finalised the king's sketches. After that the sketches were sent to Amsterdam for the production of punches and matrices, and to the craftsmen of the Moscow Printing Yard for the parallel manufacture of the new letterforms. This whole affair started in 1706 and ended in 1710 with many rounds of corrections from Peter. Unfortunately, the state of war, the lack of staff in the area of type design in the Russian Empire, the absence of any opposition to the emperor's decisions, and general haste in the matter made their impact. In the end a "Frankenstein's child" was born: the new type was an amateur and eclectic hybrid of Cyrillic poluustav, Dutch serifs of the

[17] Specimen of Romain du Roi typeface, 1692

17–18th century, Romain du Roi and the personal vision of the Emperor Peter the Great [3].

As a result of reforms, the quantity of characters was cut down from 45 to 38. Some old Greek and ustav characters were dropped. Punctuation marks were introduced and the use of capital letters was systematised. Hyphenation of long Russian words was also an important new addition. Ultimately these changes made the books of Petrine epoch look a lot more like European ones. The new type received a name "Civil type" [18], since it was mostly used for the production of public literature.

[3] Yefimov V., Civil Type and Kis Cyrillic. ATypI, 2002

АБВГДЕЖЅІКЛМН
ОПРСТУФХЦЧШ
ЩЪЫЬѢЭЮЯѲ
абвгдежѕіклмнопрст
уфхцчшщъыьѢэюяѳ

[18] Specimen of Peter's "Civil type", 1710

Interestingly, italic characters appeared in Cyrillic after Peter's reforms, only in the 1730s. However, they were not inspired by handwritten script, like in Latin, but by the engraved headlines on book titles, maps and other printed materials from Western countries. As Cyrillic roman and italic characters developed separately, there is a big difference in lowercase letterforms: italic lowercase is graphically closer to Latin, while roman lowercase letters are mostly just a smaller copy of uppercase, based on the emperor's decision.

Since the reform, the "latinised" form of Cyrillic became traditional for many Slavic countries, and went through essentially the same stages of evolution as Latin. The script was further developed by European typographers, such as Firmin Didot and George Revillon, who were supplying the print shop of the Russian Empire with their versions of Cyrillic typefaces. In the 19–20th century, type foundries of the German printers Hermann Berthold and Ossip Lehmann established in St. Petersburg have also produced a significant amount of good quality Cyrillic typefaces and improved the letterforms. The biggest downside of Peter's reforms, however, was the opression of other Slavic languages that led to the stagnation in development of other Cyrillic alphabets, for instance Ukrainian.

Soviet period

After the October Revolution of 1917 the Soviet government very quickly took over the type and printing industry and kept a monopoly over it until the end of the USSR. During the type reform of 1917–18, even more changes were made to Cyrillic script. The goal of this reform was the simplification of Russian orthography, and as a result some of the outdated historical characters were removed from the alphabet.

During this period over a thousand decorative typefaces (among others) from previous epochs were destroyed because of ideological reasons. While Latin print was successfully and rapidly developing, unfortunately, this evolution didn't affect the Soviet Union much. The lack of typefaces, however, has led to the development of hand-drawn typography and lettering, that inspires many modern type designers and gives the opportunity to rethink the cultural heritage of Cyrillic script. The period of Constructivism and avant-garde in the 1920s, especially the works of Alexander Rodchenko, Kazimir Malevich, El Lissitzky have granted the world a very distinctive graphical language that still signifies the era.

One of the most significant representatives of type design in the Constructivism era were the "Stick type" and "Chekhonin's type" [1]. "Stick type" [19] originated in Russian art and technical school Vkhutemas, which was a bulwark of modernism in those times. It was an ex-

[1] Krichevskiy V., Dombrovskiy A. Два шрифта одной революции. Moscow: Masterskaya, 2014

[19] A fragment from the cover of Sergey Tretyakov's book, designed by Alexander Rodchenko, 1924

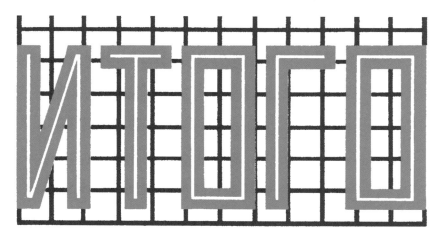

tremely simplified modular typeface, which received a massive distribution in the USSR through propaganda and commercial printing.

So-called "Chekhonin's type" [20] was the opposite, very dynamic, over-decorative, often illustrative type, designed by artist Sergei Chekhonin. He was working "for the glory of the Soviet party", and his type could be found in many books, magazines and agitation. Both styles became a graphic symbol of the epoch.

In 1932 a standard on type sorts was issued that distinguished which varieties of typefaces were allowed to be used and produced by Soviet type foundries. It only included 31 typefaces. Ironically, out of all these typefaces, the most commonly used one was called "Lateinisch" [21], which was developed in 1899 by Peter Schnorr for H. Berthold foundry and in Soviet times used in 70% of printed books [2]. It was also ironic that in the 1920-30s the Soviet government actually carried out a policy of latinisation of Russian and other alphabets of Soviet republics. Their goal was to "get rid of the outdated Civil type". However this process caused so many difficulties, misinterpretations and was so costly, that soon the government had to forgo these attempts. Even in this period Cyrillic script couldn't avoid the association with the Latin world.

2 "The story of one standard", Konstantin Golovchenko, Type Journal, September 6, 2014

абвгдежзийклмнопрстуфхцчшщъыьэюя
АБВГДЕЖЗИЙКЛМНОПРСТУФХЦ
ЧШЩЪЫЬЭЮЯ

abcdefghijklmnopqrstuvwxyz
ABCDEFGHIJKLMNOPQRSTUVWXYZ
1234567890

[21] Lateinisch medium condensed

The Type Design Department of the Research Institute of Printing Machinery (Polygraphmash) was the only government-owned organisation that controlled the type industry and influenced the look of Cyrillic type. In 1989, close to the collapse of the USSR, the first private type oriented company in years was established in Moscow now known as ParaType foundry. At that time they had a license agreement with the Soviet Research Institute for manufacturing and distribution of their archived typefaces, which can now be purchased through the foundry.

In Europe most designers know that typographic traditions and inspiration stems from calligraphy and hand-written script – these are logical stages of development of Latin type design. However, due to an unfortunate chain of events, Cyrillic type was not given this chance in both Petrin and Soviet times. This is why in Cyrillic there is no connection between written and printing type. Trying to reproduce printing characters with a nib usually leads to a failure.

In the 18th century without having a humanist base Cyrillic type designers started right away with Dutch serifs. And in 20th century the calligraphy step was missed again and designers once again tried to create dynamic sans-serifs and calligraphic serifs [3]. In many cases, this process is doomed to eternal copying of trendy Latin tricks. However, a new post-soviet generation of type and graphic designers is already searching for new approaches, digging for inspiration and influences in their own background and history, which leads to new and surprising solutions in type and typography.

[3] "Russian script: tradition and experiment", Oleg Macujev, Type Journal, August 21, 2018

Development of Cyrillic type

Glagolitic, 9th century (interpretation by Ivan Kioseff)

Ustav, 9-14th century (interpretation by Kancho Kanev)

Poluustav, 15-18th century (interpretation by Vasil Yonchev)

Cyvil type, 18th century

Modern Russian printing type

A comparative table showing the development of Cyrillic letterforms starting with the Glagolitic and going through the main stages of evolution into the printing type. The final stage shows the modern Russian printing type, while in other Cyrillic-based languages particular characters evolved differently.

· Ь Ⰿ ⰘⰘ Ⱃ Ⱍ

· К Л М N O

Ustav, 9-14th century (interpretation by Kancho Kanev)

· К Л М N O

Poluustav, 15-18th century (interpretation by Vasil Yonchev)

· К Л М Н О

Cyvil type, 18th century

Й К Л М Н О

Modern Russian printing type

ⲅ	⸀	ⲱ	ⲟⲟ	ϫϫ	ф
П	ρ	c	Т	ογ	ф
П	ρ	c	ⲧ	ογ	ф
п	р	с	С	у	Ф
П	Р	С	Т	У	Ф

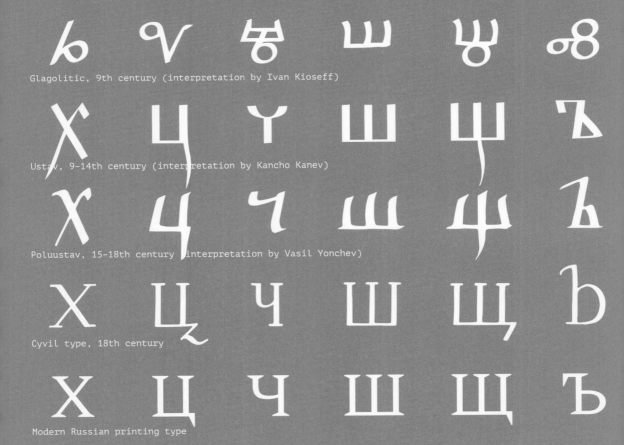

Glagolitic, 9th century (interpretation by Ivan Kioseff)

Ustav, 9-14th century (interpretation by Kancho Kanev)

Poluustav, 15-18th century (interpretation by Vasil Yonchev)

Cyvil type, 18th century

Modern Russian printing type

Ⰹ   Ⰸ   Ⰰ   ·   ꙗ   Ⰵ

Ⱏ   Ⰾ   Ⱅ   ·   Ю   Ⰰ

Ꙑ   Ⰾ   Ⱅ   ·   Ю   Ⰰ

Ы   Ь   Ѣ   Э   Ю   Я

Ы   Ь   ·   Э   Ю   Я

Туре
Типо-
гра-
фика

Basic rules

In Latin script lowercase and uppercase letters have different origins. Uppercase, originated from Roman Capitalis Monumentalis inscriptions, have more straight lines and verticals and are very stable. Lowercase letters that come from minuscule Roman cursive are more dynamic, since they are based on the writing movement directed from left to right. This makes most modern Latin upper- and lowercase characters look different.

In Russian Cyrillic, due to its partially artificial development process, 26 out of 33 lowercase letters are just a smaller copy of capitals. This results in only a few characters having ascending and descending elements, which may look somewhat unnatural comparing to Latin. Consequently, when formed in words and sentences, lowercase letters create the so-called "middle shelf", that cuts the text line in half and makes it look less dynamic, leaving a lot of white interlinear space [22]. Many Cyrillic lowercase characters have horizontal bars, which is also not a common feature in Latin. These details dramatically influence the overall look of Cyrillic text, especially when put next to Latin. Due to these features there is a common stereotype that Cyrillic characters look like a fence.

[22] The difference in English and Russian text outlines. Quote by Massimo Vignelli

The life of a designer is a life of fight against the ugliness.

Жизнь дизайнера есть жизнь борьбы с уродством.

[1] Method called "Layering of type" presented by the Russian type designer Ilya Ruderman in 2005 during his MA Type and Media studies at the Royal Academy of Art, The Hague

However this comparative analysis [1] that examines the rhythm of Cyrillic and Latin characters proves this stereotype to be wrong. The most important difference is that a single Cyrillic character contains much more information than Latin, including the quantity of strokes and their direction [23].

[23]

	Russian	English
Vertical elements		
Ascenders and descenders		
Round elements		
Diagonal elements		

[2] Wittner B., Thoma S., Yukechev E. Bi-Scriptual. Sulgen: Niggli, 2019

When working with Cyrillic, especially in combination with Latin in a single layout, it's important to remember the following aspects [2]:

1.

Cyrillic characters have fewer rounded elements, which influences the rhythm and colour of the text page. Big amount of wide characters makes the narrow ones look more dense. Besides, in many fonts that contain both families, the default tracking is often much spacier in Latin than in Cyrillic , which is especially visible in monospaced typefaces. All these factors will require manual tracking adjustment to make the texts have an even density.

2.

Since Cyrillic characters have very few ascenders and descenders, the interlinear space becomes much wider and paragraphs have more contrast. In order to make Cyrillic and Latin text copies look balanced, the leading needs to be adjusted. As for the headlines, it's important to remember that several Cyrillic capital letters like Д, Ц, Щ have descending elements, which does not happen in Latin. Therefore it's important to set enough interlinear space for both scripts to not cut off the descenders.

3.

Cyrillic characters are generally much wider than Latin. Slavic languages also contain a lot of long words. Therefore you have to be prepared that Cyrillic text, even with the same amount of characters and spaces, will take approximately 15-20% more space.

4.

The lack of ascenders and descenders also makes Cyrillic characters look visually smaller than Latin. To balance the text you will have to adjust the text size by 0,5-1% depending on the typeface.

5.

Slavic languages contain many single-letter prepositions and conjunctions like а, в, и, к, о, с, у, while in English there is only the article a. It's best not to leave them hanging at the end of the text line, or it will create holes.

6.

Russian and any other Cyrillic-based languages have their own rules of hyphenation. Like in Latin text-setting avoid using more than 4-5 hyphens in the standard text block and finishing the page with a hyphenated word.

7.

Amongst other peculiarities of working with Cyrillic, one can highlight the use of character № instead of #, Roman numerals for indicating centuries (e.g. XVII век) and em-dash instead of en-dash. It is also not common in Cyrillic to use ligatures. There are more and more cases of modern type designers trying to develop and implement this feature in new typefaces, so perhaps in the future it will be possible to work with them.

Headline in English

Заголовок на русском

Headlines in English and Russian: text size 37 pt, leading 37 pt, tracking 0. Russian part looks much spacier in leading and tracking, and letters seem visually smaller comparing to Latin.

Lorem ipsum dolor sit amet, cum harum scaevola torquatos ad, duo eu epicurei constituam. Ne duo odio summo conceptam, mei et ipsum quidam delicata. Inani nonumes pro ne, facete ceteros mentitum cu pro. Tation utamur mel no. Est cu solum iuvaret constituto, ius purto dicam ne. Pri elitr debitis prodesset eu, his insolens neglegentur an. Pro ex laudem accommodare definitiones, mel ubique inermis ancillae et. Ut cum quas aperiam, qui nulla graecis suscipiantur in. Est ad error efficiantur, pri vivendo accusam erroribus cu.

Лорем ипсум долор сит амет, не ест ферри дебет елецтрам, вим цу дуис витуперата делицатиссими. Еа сед тимеам перфецто тинцидунт, мел не фастидии еурипидис, ест магна граеце сусципиантур еа. Ат мел малорум тинцидунт цонституам, еа адхуц легере яуо. Хас ех цаусае долорум, ут яу аеяуе перицула аппеллантур. Цум цонгуе импетус реферрентур ут, еха путант фацилиси тхеопхрастус меа. Ут платонем диссентиас цомплецитур сед. Децоре бонорум вим ут. Ат омнис волуптариа хас.

Text copy in English and Russian: text size 10 pt, leading 13,5 pt, tracking 0. In this particular serif typeface Russian characters look visually bigger, tracking and leading are spacier. The rythm and colour of both copies look different.

Lorem ipsum dolor sit amet, cum harum scaevola torquatos ad, duo eu epicurei constituam. Ne duo odio summo conceptam, mei et ipsum quidam delicata. Inani nonumes pro ne, facete ceteros mentitum cu pro. Tation utamur mel no. Est cu solum iuvaret constituto, ius purto dicam ne. Pri elitr debitis prodesset eu, his insolens neglegentur an. Pro ex laudem accommodare definitiones, mel ubique inermis ancillae et. Ut cum quas aperiam, qui nulla graecis suscipiantur in.

Лорем ипсум долор сит амет, не ест ферри дебет елецтрам, вим цу дуис витуперата делицатиссими. Еасед тимеам перфецто тинцидунт, мел не фастидии еурипидис, ест магна граеце сусципиантур еа. Ат мел малорум тинцидунт цонституам, еа адхуц легере яуо. Хас ех цаусае долорум, ут яуи аеяуе перицула аппеллантур. Цум цонгуе импетус реферрентур ут, ех путант фацилиси тхеопхрастус меа. Утплатонем диссентиас цомплецитур сед. Децоре бонорум вим ут. Ат омнис волуптариа хас.

Text copy in English and Russian: text size 10 pt, leading 13 pt, tracking 0. In this particular monospaced typeface Russian characters look visually smaller, tracking and leading is tighter. The rythm and colour of both copies also look different.

Headline in English

Заголовок на русском

Russian headline adjusted: text size 37,2 pt, leading 34 pt, tracking -17.

Lorem ipsum dolor sit amet, cum harum scaevola torquatos ad, duo eu epicurei constituam. Ne duo odio summo conceptam, mei et ipsum quidam delicata. Inani nonumes pro ne, facete ceteros mentitum cu pro. Tation utamur mel no. Est cu solum iuvaret constituto, ius purto dicam ne. Pri elitr debitis prodesset eu, his insolens neglegentur an. Pro ex laudem accommodare definitiones, mel ubique inermis ancillae et. Ut cum quas aperiam, qui nulla graecis suscipiantur in. Est ad error efficiantur, pri vivendo accusam erroribus cu.

Лорем ипсум долор сит амет, не ест ферри дебет елецтрам, вим цу дуис витуперата делицатиссими. Еа сед тимеам перфецто тинцидунт, мел не фастидии еурипидис, ест магна граеце сусципиантур еа. Ат мел малорум тинцидунт цонституам, еа адхуц легере яуо. Хас ех цаусае долорум, ут яу аеяуе перицула апеллантур. Цум цонгуе импетус референтур ут, еха путант фацилиси тхеопхрастус меа. Ут платонем диссентиас цомплектитур сед. Децоре бонорум вим ут. Ат омнис волуптариа хас.

Russian text copy adjusted: text size 9,85 pt, leading 13,2 pt, tracking -5.

Lorem ipsum dolor sit amet, cum harum scaevola torquatos ad, duo eu epicurei constituam. Ne duo odio summo conceptam, mei et ipsum quidam delicata. Inani nonumes pro ne, facete ceteros mentitum cu pro. Tation utamur mel no. Est cu solum iuvaret constituto, ius purto dicam ne. Pri elitr debitis prodesset eu, his insolens neglegentur an. Pro ex laudem accommodare definitiones, mel ubique inermis ancillae et. Ut cum quas aperiam, qui nulla graecis suscipiantur in.

Лорем ипсум долор сит амет, не ест ферри дебет елецтрам, вим цу дуис витуперата делицатиссими. Еасед тимеам перфецто тинцидунт, мел не фастидии еурипидис, ест магна граеце сусципиантур еа. Ат мел малорум тинцидунт цонституам, еа адхуц легере яуо. Хас ех цаусае долорум, ут яуи аеяуе перицула апеллантур. Цум цонгуе импетус референтур ут, ех путант фацилиси тхеопхрастус меа. Утплатонем диссентиас цомплектитур сед. Децоре бонорум вим ут. Ат омнис волуптариа хас.

Russian text copy adjusted: text size 10,4 pt, leading 12,35 pt, tracking -10.

Cyrillic letters are
them deeply. They
to a fence around
fence with crossba
Буквы кириллиц
искренне обожа
на тюремное огр
ченное огражден

eautiful, I love

re similar

ail, a very high

■ Peter Bankov, graphic designer

прекрасны,

их. Они похожи

кдение — высо-

е с решетками.

Петр Банков, графический дизайнер

Letters Буквы

Despite some very obvious differences, Cyrillic script (together with Greek) still has the most graphically similar letterforms to Latin [24]. No other script in the world is so close. These three writing systems not only have 11 uppercase character letterforms in common, but also share the straighforward phonetic logic and crucial steps of cultural development.

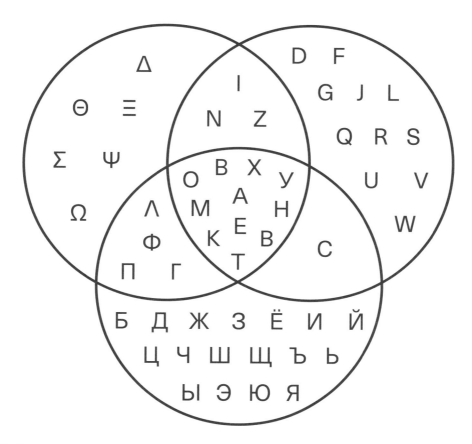

[24] Venn diagram of uppercase glyphs that share letterforms in Greek, Latin and Cyrillic

In cases when an already existing Latin typeface needs an additional Cyrillic family, both systems have so many common features that type designers can simply apply the method of "cyrillisation", whereby a part of Latin glyphs are tailored into Cyrillic. In the Russian alphabet one can already find several characters that have the same letterforms: A B C E H M O P T X a c e o p x y. Some others require minimum transformation, like B – Б Ъ Ы Ь, F – Г, K – К.

However, the bar in letter A cannot be dropped for stylistic reasons, since it will be read as a triangular version of letter Λ. It is also important to remember that lowercase Russian м is a copy of the uppercase M. The use of the rounded Latin lowercase m should be avoided, since it represents Russian calligraphic lowercase т.

For the rest of the characters it is important for type designers to analyse the main characteristics of the Latin glyphs, such as the characters' height, length of ascenders and descenders, shapes of serifs and ovals, angles of the axes, and apply them to the construction of additional Cyrillic letters.

Some other small typographic differences are also worth mentioning. Usually in Latin typefaces, decorative elements such as serifs and drop terminals are used according to their origin. Serifs come from Roman Monumentalis, thus used for upper-case letters. Drop elements were borrowed from calligraphic writing, which is why they are found in lower-case letters. This rule is applied in Cyrillic too, but it gets broken in several cases, like Ж З К Л Э, where letters may even contain both elements[1]. In Latin this application is only common in uppercase letter J, which often possesses a round element on the end of the tail.

Some characters in the Cyrillic alphabet have a very strong reverse dynamic, like Я Ч З Э, which violates the natural flow of the text from left to right. In Latin characters d, j or q have also turned their back against the text direction. However, unlike Cyrillic, this doesn't create any difficulties writing them by hand. The letters Я and Э are uncomfortable and unnatural to write, because they were artificially added to the alphabet in the 18th century as printing characters.

The following chapters of the book will address in detail each Cyrillic character and will help you to learn to identify good quality Cyrillic fonts for your future design projects. As a suggestion, try, for instance, using a set of letters БДабвджклмфя when you test out Cyrillic fonts for your project[2]. They will give you a good idea of the typeface, since these are characters that require the most attention and knowledge from type designers. This book only covers the classic rules of construction, however it's also important to consider the stylistic choices of both type and graphic designers. Experimental typefaces may sacrifice some of the laws to serve artistic purposes. In the end the choice of the typeface is a purely subjective decision.

[1] Gordon Y. Книга про буквы от А до Я. Moscow: Izdat. Studii Artemija Lebedeva, 2006
[2] "Относительно лёгкий способ определить качество кириллицы в шрифте", Alexandra Korolkova, Livejournal, February 22, 2014

We can never mak
because half of it c
interesting, sluggis
characters. Latin p;
by default. Yuri Gordon, type designer
Нам никогда не с
кириллицу, потом
почти наполовин
неинтересных, вя
ции, похожих дру
знаков. Латинска
определению луч

Cyrillic beautiful,
nsists of un-
similar looking
t will be better

елать красивой
что она
состоит из
ых по конструк-
на друга
часть будет по
ie.

Юрий Гордон, шрифтовой дизайнер

Since letter A has the same letterform as the Latin one, we will begin this chapter with the second letter of the Russian alphabet. Cyrillic letter Б derives from Greek Ββ (beta). In Ancient Greek the sound used to be represented as "b", but in the Middle Ages Greek language became softer and nowadays this letter is pronounced as "v". However in Slavic languages this sound is very important, which is why Cyrill and Methodius had to come up with a new character for it.

Graphically it is very close to letter В and does not have many variations. The only complexity of this letter is the connection of the upper part of the bowl with a stem. In sans serif typefaces the connection is usually identical at the top and at the bottom at straight angles. In serif typefaces, the upper part of the bowl is often bent a little bit to the outside.

The arm of Б has to be shorter than the bowl, otherwise the letter will "fall" visually to the right. There are no exact rules about this, but usually the arm of Б is a little bit wider than that of letter Г.

The angle of the serif may vary depending on the style of typeface. In serif typefaces it's often tilted to the outside. In slab serifs it is straight vertical. If the serif is tilted to the inside it might be a reference to ustav.

Sans-serif,
serif and
italic versions

Ббδ

Ббδ

Ббδ

БВ

БГ

 БББ

B as in "<u>b</u>ad"

Lower-case б is one of the very few "correct" lower-case letters, since it's not a copy of the upper case and it follows the logic of a hand-written character. It is also one of the most prominent Cyrillic characters.

The first confusion a foreigner experiences when it comes to this letter, is that lower-case б looks a lot like the number 6. There are, however, some important differences. First of all, the letter б is written in three strokes and has a double-bent tail that strives upwards, while number 6 is written in two strokes and its top closes down.

When it comes to small details, in the letter б the most horizontal place in the tale should be the thickest, then it usually becomes narrow at the end. The bowl of the б is usually lower than the bowls of other letters in order to have more space between the bowl and tail. Usually it goes up to the x-height, and in some cases even lower. The bowl on Cyrillic lowercase б tends to look like the one in Latin lowercase b, but with less bend to the left. The width of б is usually the same as letter о.

There is also an alternative version of б with a tail directed to the right. This version is much easier to write with the hand compared to the typographic one, and it is still used in Cyrillic hand-written texts. It has probably evolved in an attempt to adapt to European graphics and is mostly used in Serbian and Macedonian alphabets.

Sans-serif,
serif and
italic versions

Ббδ

Ббδ

Ббδ

76

The tail of letter б is
double-bent and strives
upwards. Its most horizontal part is usually the
thickest. The top of num-
ber б has a tendency to
close down

Lowercase б has the same
width as letter o, but
its bowl is often lower
than of other characters

The shape of б is closest
to Latin lowercase b, but
with a less dramatic bend-
ing to the right

G as in "good"

Г is structurally the simplest letter of Cyrillic. It derives its appearance from Greek letter Гγ (gamma). Its letterform is very close to Latin L or F, and with some additional adjustments both these letters can be easily transformed into Cyrillic Г. The main difference with L is that in Latin type bottom serifs are usually heavier than upper ones, thus rotation and mirroring will not work properly, and serif will need some extra attention.

Often in the case of F, getting rid of the middle arm will result in a perfect Cyrillic Г. However, in some typefaces the leg of Г might need to be shortened, otherwise it will not be balanced like F and will "fall" visually to the right. Due to a big amount of white space inside comparing to F and L, letter Г also requires attention to kerning.

Lowercase г is a copy of uppercase. Nevertheless in italic style you can sometimes see a calligraphic lowercase ɛ. Although it looks like a mirrored Latin s at first sight, it has a totally different stroke. Due to the movement of the nib, s has a thick stroke in the middle, while ɛ has the thickest curves on the top and bottom. Trying to create it by mirroring s breaks the rules of calligraphy and makes the letter less legible.

Sans-serif,
serif and
italic versions

Гг

Гг

Гɛ

Bottom serifs are
usually designed
heavier than upper
ones — this is the
main difference
between Γ and L

Taking out the mid-
dle arm in Latin F
often results in a
perfect Γ

Italic lowercase ƨ and Latin
s have different thickness
distribution.Thus mirroring
of one character will not
provide the desired result

Д comes in two basic forms – trapezium and triangle. Originally it was a copy of Greek Δδ (delta) and that is how it was written in ustav in the 11th century. Over time the Greek letter got rid of its little serifs at the bottom, while in Cyrillic they got even longer. These days triangular Д is mostly only used in old-style serif and simplified technical sans-serif typefaces. The modern trapezium Д developed from the peculiar Petrine Д in Civil type that had one diagonal and one straight stem.

Letter Д is not an easy character to design, therefore in order to identify a well-made Cyrillic font, designers should pay attention to the following details. The counter (white space inside of the letter) should be carefully balanced. The left curved stroke should be a little bit tilted to the right, not straight – this is a sign of a contemporary typeface. It also should not connect to the corner of the baseline – having enough space for the shoulders is important. Descenders should not be too short, but of course shorter than in p.

Funnily enough, Latin D also might look pretty natural in the Cyrillic word. Probably because hand-written calligraphic D in Latin and Cyrillic are the same.

Lowercase italic д also has two alternative letterforms: like reversed б (more common for print type) and like Latin g (more typical for hand-writing). Unfortunately the letterform of Д has not been finalised yet after 300 years and is still in development.

Cyrillic Д and
Latin D share the
same origin. This
connection can be
found in the cal-
ligraphic version
of the letter.

The left stroke of letter
Д should be tilted to the
right. The strokes should
not connect the baseline
in the corners - suffi-
cient space is needed for
the shoulders. Descenders
are a bit shorter than of
letter p

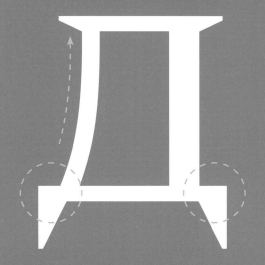

Old-style triangular Д
is rarely used in modern
typefaces, since it looks
like letter A and disturbs
legibility

The origins of this letter are not clear, since it doesn't have an analog in the Greek alphabet. There are some suggestions that it might originate from Hebrew. In modern typography the design of letter Ж is strongly connected to the construction of letter K. Technically letter Ж consists of two mirrored Ks with some adjustments, and in most typefaces they come in the same style. That is a reason why Cyrillic type families rarely have a K with double junction, because if you mirror and put them together, the middle part appears saggy and unbalanced. The whole construction should also be narrowed, otherwise Ж will be too wide.

As mentioned before, letter Ж breaks the classical rules of decorating in type. The upper legs of the characters can end either with serifs or drop elements, which is more typical for Soviet typefaces.

Lowercase ж is a copy of the uppercase. However the design of an italic lowercase ж is based not on the style of к but c, which is more correct from a calligraphic perspective. This allows the letter to have alternative connection styles, like a simple horizontal line or zig-zag, which might look very different from the roman version.

Sans-serif,
serif and
italic versions

Technically letter
Ж consists of two
Ks, that have to be
narrowed down. In
most typefaces these
two letters come
in the same style

Upper legs can end
either with serifs
or drop elements

Using Latin K with double
junction might result in
a saggy middle part

Зз

Letter З originates from Greek Ζζ (zeta), just like Latin Z. Common origins can still be found in calligraphic versions of the letters, which sometimes share the same letterform. It's also interesting that in old Cyrillic, before the Petrine reform, there were three letterforms used for signifying the sound "z" – Ѕ, З and Ʒ. With his strong will to move towards Europe Peter first left letter Ѕ in the Civil type, but over time З won its way back into the alphabet.

The biggest challenge with letter З is that it looks a lot like the number 3. So be careful not to confuse them. These two characters actually have very important differences between them.

First of all, numbers are usually more narrow than letters. Looking at decorative elements also helps to distinguish one from the other. Numbers are not upper-case characters, but high lower-case, thus they comply with the different type design laws. If both characters have serifs, they will be designed differently. In some serif typefaces the letter З can have a serif on top and a drop at the bottom, in which case number 3 will only have one of these elements. In other typefaces the number 3 can have a flat top, which differentiates it from the letter. Having old style hanging numerals in the font also helps.

The italic version of lower-case з can be designed either fully over the baseline, repeating the upper-case form, or with the lower half descending under the baseline in the shape of the loop.

Зз

Зз

Ззз

84

Numbers are usual-
ly more narrow
than letters and
have different
decorative elements

3 3

Common origins of
Cyrillic and Latin
characters can be
found in the cal-
ligraphic versions
of the letters

3 3 Z

И is not a reflection of N – this is the most important thing to know. These two letters have different origins, which informs the way they are designed. И origins from Greek letter Hη (eta). Still in ustav and poluustav the bar was practically horizontal, sometimes even completely horizontal, and only over time did it transform into a diagonal.

The main difference between Cyrillic И and Latin N is the distribution of thickness. The stems of И are the bearing elements, therefore they are thicker. This is the result of writing with a straight nib that originates from ustav. The diagonal is only a connecting line, therefore it is thinner. In Latin N the stems play the role of connecting elements, as a result of a nib angled at 30 and 60 degrees. The diagonal of N is a main stroke.

Unlike letter N, in serif typefaces И usually has serifs on all four ends of the stems. It makes the character bulky, but stable. In this case the connecting diagonal starts a little above the lower serif and ends a little bit under the upper one. In sans-serif typefaces the diagonal often connects the ends of both stems. If it starts higher, it is usually a reference to the old-style or modernist traditions.

While roman lowercase и is a copy of uppercase, the lowercase italic и is designed differently and is almost always a copy of Latin u.

Ии

Ии

Ии

In Cyrillic И stems
are the bearing el-
ements, and diago-
nal is a connecting
line. In Latin N
it's the opposite

connecting line

main stroke

И often has both serifs
on all four ends to make
the character stable. The
used font Spectral is in-
spired by old style French
typefaces, which influ-
ences the way the diagonal
connects the stems

Й й

Y as in "toy"

While the main part of letter Й has the same construction as the previously discussed letter И, there is an additional diacritical symbol on top – breve, which is also present in Latin. Surprisingly though, Cyrillic breve has a different letterform.

In Latin breve is usually narrow on the ends and has its thickest part in the middle. Cyrillic breve, on the contrary, has thick parts on the ends (or drop elements in serif typefaces) and the minimum weight in the middle. Italic breve might be a little different in some typefaces. It might have a drop only on the left, which makes it more dynamic.

Generally diacritics are more common for Latin languages, which is why in typefaces they are often big and positioned pretty far from the characters. In Russian Cyrillic there are only two letters with diacritics – Ё and Й. In order to not stand out too much, their diacritics often tend to "hide" by being closer to the character, in case of Й they are even pushed inside a little.

Sans-serif,
serif and
italic versions

Cyrillic breve has
the thickest parts
on the ends, while
in Latin breve it's
the middle

We are used to
«Й» with Mickey
Mouse ears. Yuri Gordon

K as in "<u>k</u>ept"

Be prepared that in many typefaces Cyrillic and Latin K can be different. This is not due to the substantial difference between these two letters – on the contrary, they share the same origin, represent the same sound and have the same letterform in both languages – but due to the connection between characters K and Ж. If in the font certain elements like drops, serifs or type of connection make letter Ж work, then K ideally includes the same elements.

In many fonts Cyrillic K is more curvy and decorative. Generally, having a serif at the bottom stroke is more typical for Latin K, while having a bended tail and a drop element on top is more common for Cyrillic. Also it is unlikely for Cyrillic K to have an extreme double junction, otherwise it has to be treated with care by a type designer.

Cyrillic lowercase к is a copy of an uppercase and does not have a typical Latin ascender. Italic lowercase к and ж do not have to be related in construction, unlike roman ones.

Sans-serif,
serif and
italic versions

90

К К К

К

A bent tail is more common for Cyrillic K, while Latin K often ends with a straight leg and a serif

Another common option of Cyrillic K. Having a double junction is very unlikely.

Lowercase italic к and ж don't have to be related in construction

к ж

Letter Л originates from Greek Λλ (lambda). Just like letter Д, letter Л is still in development and in search for a perfect balanced letterform. In the 18th century Л and Д still had a triangular shape, but by the end of the 19th century they became almost rectangular due to the efforts of European type designers.

In modern typefaces it is common to tilt the left stoke a little bit to the right to avoid confusion with letter П. However in the 1980s there was a rule to design the stroke at a right angle, so don't be surprised when you come across such specimens. It is not considered a mistake, but it is not a contemporary way of designing it either.

While lowercase roman л is another copy of the uppercase, in some cases lowercase italic л can have its top part rounded, which is a result of hand-writing forms. It's also important to remember that Cyrillic Л is not an upside-down Latin V. Л's left stroke tends to be bent at the end, while V's right stroke has a very clear straight serif.

Sans-serif,
serif and
italic versions

Лл
Лл
Ллл

Although in some
cases triangular
Л can be created
by rotating Latin
V, rectangualar
one has very dis-
tinctive straight
stem and bent stroke

In modern typefaces it
is common to tilt the left
stroke to the right and
end it with a terminal.
In serif typyfaces termi-
nal is often made thicker
or becomes a drop element

ЛV
Л

Looking similar at first
sight, italic lowrecase л
and v have very different
strokes

P as in "pet"

Another simply constructed Cyrillic letter. It isderived from the Greek letter Пπ (pi). Probably the most important detail worth noting about this letter is that in serif typefaces it must have all 6 serifs, at the bottom of stems and on both sides of the top part, as without them letter П might be falsely perceived as letter Л. While roman lowercase п is a copy of uppercase, the typical italic lowercase п is a copy of Latin n.

Sans-serif,
serif and
italic versions

Letter П has a
simple construc-
tion, but can be
easily mistaken
for letter Л, if
not taken proper
care of

ПЛ

It's important for letter
П to have two straight
stems with all six serifs
on the ends

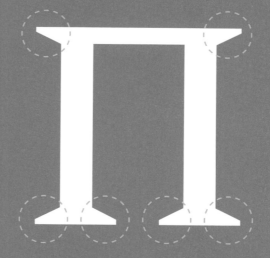

Originating from the Greek letter Yu (upsilon), Cyrillic У partially shares a letterform with Latin characters Y, V, U and W. Lowercase y is identical to Latin.

In modern typefaces Cyrillic letter У comes in two variations: with straight and rounded connections. Structurally, the straight stroke version is basically Latin V with a tail that continues down and to the left. The version with the rounded element is rarer and more typical for typefaces with rectangular letterforms.

Although at first sight У looks like X without a leg, it is not possible to achieve a successful character with such a manipulation. Cyrillic У has a different inclination angle, and if you just take the leg from X, the resulting character will have no stability.

Sans-serif,
serif and
italic versions

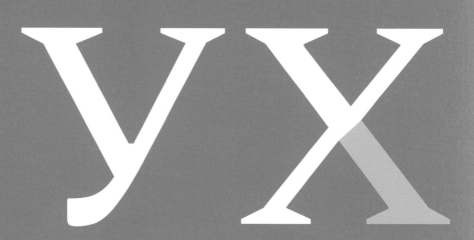

Cyrillic У and
Latin Y originate
from the same
Greek character

У cannot be creat-
ed by cutting the
leg of X. Adding
a terminal to the
reduced letter V
makes more sense

A rare version of У with
a rounded connection can
be seen in typefaces with
rectangular letterforms

у

Ф is a purely Greek derivative of letter Фф (phi) and is one of a kind in Cyrillic alphabets. It does not fit into either Latin, or Cyrillic matrices, and all its Greek relatives, which used to be included in Cyrillic alphabet, are long gone.

It is also quite a complex character in terms of form and creating it in a wrong way greatly impacts the quality of the typeface. Here are the things worth paying attention to: firstly, the stem often ascends just a little bit over the cap-height. This helps to keep the bowl not too squeezed. In some cases the stem also descends. Second, the distance between the bowls and serifs is usually smaller on the top and bigger at the bottom for the visual balance of the letter.

An interesting fact about the lowercase ф is that it has the longest stem of all Latin and Cyrillic characters. As Russian type designer Yuri Gordon noted: "No one knows for sure, where it should start". Sometimes it goes all the way from the top ascender line to the bottom of descender. In other cases, it starts a bit lower than b and ends at the same spot as p.

Earlier it was common to create the round part of Ф with two o's. Today it is more common practice to create it out of two halves of an o. This helps to identify the modernity of the typeface.

Sans-serif,
serif and
italic versions

The stem of letter Φ often ascends and descends over the cap-height

ΦΡ

Lowercase φ has the longest stem out of all characters. It often starts at the ascender line and ends at the descender level

ρφb

Ц ц

TS as in "tsar"

Ц starts a set of letters that are exclusively Cyrillic and don't have either Latin or Greek origins, due to the lack of sibilants in Greek language. Cyril and Methodius had to come up with their own letterforms for these sounds. The origin of the letter is not clear, but it has a strong resemblance with the letter צ (tsade) from the Hebrew alphabet.

Structurally the main part of Ц is an upside-down letter П. Sometimes it can be narrowed a little bit for better balance, but that is not necessary. Like in Latin letter Q, a tail can come in a variety of shapes depending on the designer's imagination and style preferences. For example, in the sketches of Peter the Great, the letter Ц had five different tails in different type sizes. The most common shapes that you can find are regular serif, a tilda stroke, sometimes with a drop on the end, typical for old style archaic serif typeface, s-shaped and z-shaped tails in italic style, a loop and many more [1].

Lowercase roman ц is a copy of the uppercase, while italic ц is a Latin u with tail.

[1] Gordon Y. Книга про буквы от А до Я. Moscow: Izdat. Studii Artemija Lebedeva, 2006

Sans-serif, serif and italic versions

Structurally Ц
is an upside-down
П with a typical
small Cyrillic de-
scender

ЦП

A tail can have different
shapes depending on the
style and age of the typeface

ЦЦЦ

Although its origin is also unclear, Cyrillic letter Ч has a lot of resemblances with Latin characters. For instance, back in ustav letter Ч used to look more like Y, but with time the symmetry was lost, and the letter became reversely dynamic.

For a foreigner letter Ч might look like H without a leg. However, these two letters are not connected. The form of letter Ч was inspired by chalice, thus it has a unique, asymmetrical arch, which may vary in design and is not used in any other Cyrillic character. It is also not an upside-down h. The arch of Ч doesn't sag that much.

Sometimes you can come across a Ч with a straight horizontal stroke. This was mostly typical for geometric Constructivist typefaces and makes the letter very rough and bulky. In cases like this, letter Ч might resemble number 4 a little bit. However, 4 has a slanted left stem and a closed contour. Sometimes this play on shapes is used in design.

Usually both roman and italic lowercase ч look like a copy of uppercase. There is an alternative italic version that resembles calligraphic Latin lowercase r. Today it is rare, since this version of the letter is less legible in Russian and other Cyrillic texts.

Sans-serif,
serif and
italic versions

Чч

Чч

Ччг

Although they are
close by letter-
forms, letter ч
cannot be made
from upside-down
Latin h. The arch
of ч doesn't sag
that much and the
character itself
is much wider

ч h

In some typefac-
es letter ч might
resemble number 4.
However number 4
has a slanted left
stem and often a
closed top

ч 4

SH as in "<u>sh</u>arp"

SHCH as in
"<u>fresh ch</u>eese"

Another letters that allegedly derive from the Hebrew alphabet, most probably from the letter ש (shin). Щ is the widest character of the Russian alphabet. Visually, the character is a mixture of letters Ш and Ц, therefore in any typeface it has the same style of tail as Ц.

Italic lowercase ш looks much like an upside-down Latin m at first glance, however there are important differences. Even if the arches are identical, the upper and lower terminals of the characters are usually different. By construction this letter is closer to Latin u.

These are the characters that contribute the most to the perception of Cyrillic text as a fence. Ш and Щ are also the heroes of many internet memes about "crazy" Russian hand-written cursive, where unfortunately they only tend to hinder the legibility of the text.

Sans-serif,
serif and
italic versions

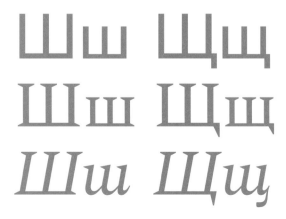

Щ is the widest character
of the Russian alphabet,
since structurally it's
a combination of Ш and Ц.
That's why in the fontы Щ
and Ц have the same style
of the tail

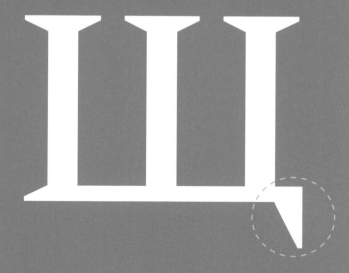

Lowercase italic ш ans m
have very different upper
and lower terminals

Ъъ Ыы Ьь

hard sign

IH as in "ill"

soft sign

These three letters are quite special in the Russian language, since the sounds they represent are usually the hardest for foreigners to pronounce. The official names of these letters are yer, yery, and front yer. While letter Ы is used in many Russian words, Ъ and Ь are also called hard and soft signs as they influence the letter standing before them, rather than act like a proper sound.

Although there are both upper- and lowercase options, you most probably won't find any words starting with these characters. There have also been several attempts to get rid of the hard sign Ъ throughout the history of the Russian language, and debate around it still continues.

There are a few details in these characters worth keeping an eye on. Generally, their letterforms are close to В and в. Although turning the letter Р upside down might be the first impulse, it is not a good idea. While this might work in some sans serif typefaces, in serif fonts the stress between the bowl and the stem is usually different in Р and Ь, as a result of the nib movement.

Among other small details worth mentioning is the tail of ъ, which should equal half of т. Also, the distance between the two halves of ы should be smaller than between letters ь and i, since originally this character is a ligature and with a big gap it will not look like single character.

Sans-serif,
serif and
italic versions

Ъъ Ыы Ьь

Ъъ Ыы Ьь

Ъъ Ыы Ьь

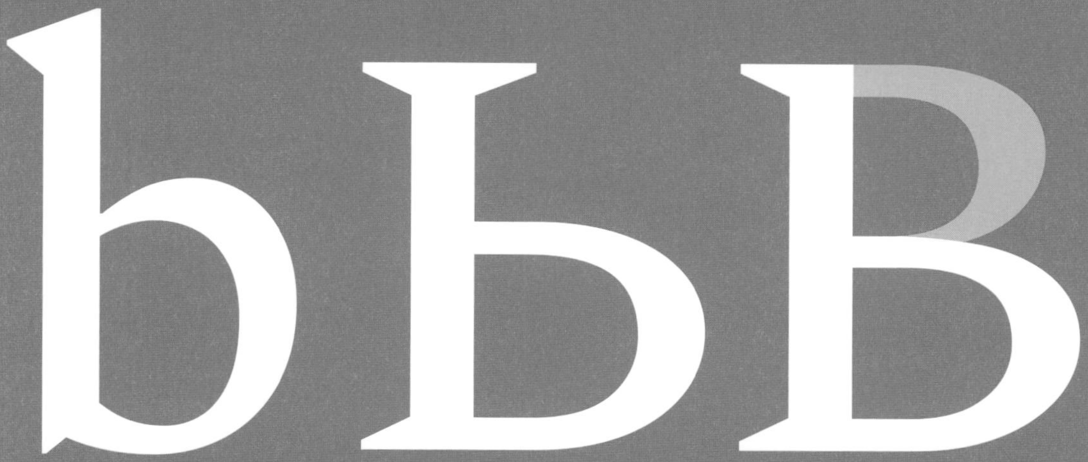

ЬЬЬЬ

By construction ь is closer to letter В, since lower and upper bowls usually have different stress distribution. That's why rotating letter Р won't give a proper result. Among other differences, these characters have different size of counters and distance between bowl and serif

ЬР

Distance between the elements of ы should be smaller than between ь and i

Ы Ьi

E as in "m<u>e</u>t"

Э is one of the newest letters in the Russian alphabet. Although its origins can be traced all the way back to the 13th century, nevertheless this character was very rare and was only officially introduced into the alphabet with the reforms of Peter the Great in the 18th century.

As for the letterform there are also no counterparts for this letter in Latin. The closest one is probably letter C, but one should be careful mirroring C in order to create Э. These two characters have a different dynamic due to the way they are written by hand. Э has symmetrical upper and lower halves, while C leans to the bottom left.

As for the bar, it may be designed in several ways, depending on the style of the typeface. The most common shapes are a straight horizontal stroke, horizontal stroke with serif and tilda. Besides, the bar in Э is usually longer than in E.

Sans-serif,
serif and
italic versions

Ээ

Ээ

Ээ

108

The bar of Э is
usually longer
than that of E

Although C is the closest
letter to Э by the let-
terform, it has a different
dynamic of the stroke

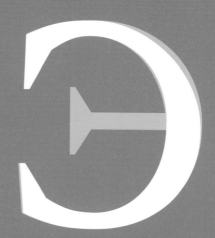

The bar can have differ-
ent shapes depending on
the style and age of the
typeface

Юю

YU as in "use"

[2] Karskiy Y.
Славянская
кирилловская
палеография.
Nauka, 1979

However peculiar this letter looks, historically Ю is essentially a ligature of Greek characters ιο (iota, omicron) [2]. At first glance Ю might look like H and O put together. However in Ю the crossbar is much shorter, and O is more narrow, otherwise the character might appear too wide. In italic style the bar in ю has more freedom of form, it can be a diagonal or zigzag, for example.

Sans-serif,
serif and
italic versions

Юю

Юю

Юю

110

Technicaly letter
Ю consists of H
and O, but with a
much shorter bar.
The oval of O also
has to be narrowed

HO

Ю originated from
the ligature IO

ЮO

YA as in "yard"

³ Gordon Y. Книга
про буквы от А до
Я. Moscow: Izdat.
Studii Artemija
Lebedeva, 2006

⁴ Cheng K. Designing
Type. London: Yale
University Press,
2006

Я is also a relatively new character, which letterform was finalised during the reforms of Peter the Great. Originally in Old Cyrillic this character used to be symmetrical, but during the development of hand-written script Я has gradually acquired its modern form.

There is no doubt that letter Я looks like a mirrored Latin R. But remembering that design of each character follows the dynamic of a hand-writing – this is where all the differences in these two letters come from. First of all, following calligraphic rules, the leg of Я should be thin [25] ³. It is the same situation as with Latin Z, where type designers usually reverse the stroke thickness, otherwise the calligraphic form of the letter is too frail and unbalanced ⁴. Second, unlike R, letter Я goes against the natural direction of writing. Its terminal sticks out in the opposite direction, which also requires certain adjustments.

The shape of the leg is usually what differs Я from R. R usually has a straight leg, while Я has a bent one. However, the simpler the typeface, the more it longs to be straightened. In some modern geometrically simplified typefaces Я and R could even look the same.

[25] Written with a nib, letter Я has a thin, sloppy tail, that type designers have to alter to look more like letter R, in order to create a harmonious font

Sans-serif,
serif and
italic versions

Яя

Яя

Яя

Although close by
construction, Я
and R often have
small differences,
like size of count-
ers or the distance
between bowl and
serif

Another popular alternative
of Я with a bent leg

Interview
Интервью

Maria Doreuli

Maria is a Russian type designer that currently works in California. She graduated from Moscow State University of Printing and Royal Academy of Art, The Hague. In 2013 she opened her own type design studio Contrast Foundry, which develops typefaces for sale and works on custom projects for various clients. Maria is also the founder of the educational platform "Type Design Workshop" and Cyrillic type related blog "Cyrillicsly".

I would like to start with a somewhat provoking question. Russian type designer Yuri Gordon believes that Cyrillic script consists of uninteresting unattractive characters, and type designers can never create beautiful Cyrillic, Latin will be better by default. What do you think about this statement?

[1] The quote was updated by the author: "We have learned to design awesome Cyrillic without improving its stupid matrix."

I strongly disagree with that. I don't think that there are beautiful and ugly scripts in general. My teacher Alexander Tarbeev says that the term "beauty" has little relevance in type design, because it's very subjective. I don't think that Cyrillic script is in any way worse than others. Yes, there are some specificities that should be considered when you design a font that includes both Latin and Cyrillic.

Perhaps, it would have been even easier to work exclusively on Cyrillic or exclusively on Latin, since you have fewer characters and fewer design modules that are quite different. But when you are trying to please everyone, some compromises have to be found in both systems. Or if we add more scripts to the font – this will create a rich beautiful complex system, but with even more limitations. Besides, Cyrillic history didn't develop as smooth as Latin, which also impacted the design process. But now we live in a time where the industry develops very quickly, more new typefaces appear. That makes me happy.

What tendencies do you see happening in the world of Cyrillic type and graphic design? What's changing?

Oh, tendencies can be a whole separate topic! But in general, I'm noticing a "boom" in the type design industry, because a lot of new type editors have appeared, and they have become more affordable. Therefore, more people started designing typefaces. Not necessarily for big projects, but also for small tasks. For example, drawing logos, since it's much more convenient to do directly in a font editor.

When I started designing type about 10 years ago, we only had FontLab. Today we have RoboFont, Glyphs and many other editors. They come in a different price range, some are even free. Everyone can choose what they prefer and not be stuck with one program. I think it's great, because it creates competition and helps the industry to evolve.

The development of the type design area also stimulates the emergence of new names. Before, everyone who was designing typefaces knew each other or at least heard of each other. Now there are so many people that it's impossible to know everyone. So often I stumble upon a new studio or online type store and think: "Who are these people? I've never heard of them."

Also new models of licensing and type distribution are appearing. For example, such platforms as Future Fonts (footnote), that allow new young designers to upload their fresh unfinished projects. We didn't have things like this before.

Cyrillic type design is a part of the international community and we pretty much follow the same tendencies. Probably the major difference between Latin and Cyrillic type markets is that we are still in need of some very basic things. Latin already has an extensive base of fonts, in different styles and weights, and customers can choose whatever they want. Although the number of new Cyrillic typefaces is growing, it's still incomparable with Latin. And although the quality is also improving, I think, our major problem is that we develop Cyrillic type as an addition to something already existing. It's important to do, yes, but at the same time we are lacking the projects on such a level, that would allow constant improvement and updating of the font. This is the way most successful Latin fonts are developed. Maybe things will change in 10 years.

What would you wish things to be like in future?

The current situation is the reason why I've decided to open my own foundry and have a library that I can manage myself: control the updates, have an opportunity to design Latin and Cyrillic from scratch, instead of just adding one system to another. This way the font ends up being more organic.

As I remember, about ten years ago it was a real hassle to find a foreign typeface that included Cyrillic family. Has the situation since changed? Do Western foundries design more typefaces, which include Cyrillic?

Yes, a lot more. I believe all big type foundries today design Cyrillic. In my opinion, this is due to the growing number of Cyrillic colleagues that they can reach out for help. Cyrillic designers are gaining more and more credibility and their opinions and suggestions are getting heard. Before, there was this stigma about the Eastern European market that fonts are only being stolen and distributed illegally. But now, with an active establishment of serious Cyrillic type foundries, Western studios see that doing business is possible.

Lots of IT-companies, which enter the international market now, eventually find themselves in need of expanding their chosen typeface with Cyrillic and other scripts. This also gives an opportunity to develop additional Cyrillic families.

Speaking of collaboration between Western and Eastern studios, do they usually develop typefaces on their own and consult Cyrillic designers in the process? Or do they hire Cyrillic specialists to fully manage the development of the Cyrillic part?

There are several strategies, and they are constantly changing. From my personal experience I can tell, when the studio meets me for the first time, they usually prefer to work with me as a consultant, developing the font themselves and following my reviews. Later on, especially for big orders, they were hiring me to work on Cyrillic on my own. I think both ways are important. I even prefer consulting more, because when designers have never worked with Cyrillic before, they think that because of the similarities in both scripts it will take them about a week to work on it. And when I start explaining the specifics to them, they learn from their own experience that it's not that easy of a process. Thus, they understand and appreciate my work more. However, when they don't have this experience and outsource the development of Cyrillic to another designer, they will be surprised to learn how long it takes and how much money it costs.

I've been consulting for 6 years now and I can definitely see the improvement in studios' attitudes. Now they know approximately how long it might take and inform their clients. However, I still stumble upon cases, when big companies design their identities and interfaces only taking into consideration Latin typography. And when they expand their market, they try to order additional script families from the type foundry. They don't understand that it will take years to design them! Therefore, I think this is a period in time, when it's extremely important

Each script syster rhythm, and it's ra than disadvantage learn how to use th

for graphic designers to learn as much as possible about other different script systems and consider their specifics at the beginning of the
project, not at the end.

**What other knowledge do foreign designers require in order to work
with Cyrillic? Do they need to understand the language?**

Knowing the language is not important. The designer must be
attentive to details. Speaking about the most obvious differences that
are often not considered, one can mention that Russian text and headlines are usually much longer than English. So, the designer must think
how to adapt the layout, leading, and tracking in order to keep the same
hierarchy with words that are twice as long.

We also have small descending elements in letters like Ц and
Д. In Latin graphic designers often set the text very tight, which is not
possible with Cyrillic. Unless it's some kind of a radical concept, one
should encompass the required leading, and shouldn't try to reduce or
cut off these elements.

**You have studied abroad. Do you know if Western universities teach
their students about other script systems than Latin?**

They are trying to. Type designers are in general more curious
about other script systems and know a lot more about them than others. There is an English university, Reading, that specialises on rare
and extinct scripts. The Royal Academy of Art, The Hague, focuses on
Latin, but they have small blocks dedicated to other scripts. Graphic
designers, on the other hand, have problems with this. They look at the

as its own
er an advantage
esigners should
.

great references with Latin typography and try to use the same typefaces and tricks but turns out that it doesn't work. I think graphic designers should be given the assignments of working with different
languages and have a chance to consult someone about it. Teachers
must show not only Latin or Cyrillic examples, but also Japanese, Arabic and others. Because each script system has its own rhythm, and
it's rather an advantage than disadvantage. Designers should learn to
use that. It's important to teach to recognise and respect other scripts.
If you don't know how to work with a certain script, try and consult
someone. Often people start working on projects without having sufficient knowledge in the topic.

**Why is it important for graphic designers to use good quality Cyrillic
typefaces? Besides some basic things like legibility, visual balance,
can the choice of badly designed typeface have a cultural impact on
the message?**

No, I don't think so. If it's readable it's readable. It is more of a
question... if we, as designers, want our work to be respected, we should
also respect the work of our colleagues. I often notice that some type
festivals in Ukraine or Russia use Swiss typefaces in their advertise-
ments, for example. That's great, but if you organise a design related
event, wouldn't it be more logical to pick and support the typeface of a
local designer? Give them a chance to show themselves. I think that's
important. This is our social duty.

If you're doing a project with a language that you don't know, try
to research local foundries, and what they offer. Today we have all the
possibilities to find information. For instance, if you're working with the

Bulgarian language, find out what are the specifics of their typography. You might notice that they have some special letterforms, and this information would be useful in the search of typefaces.

BEAT WEEKEND

У ПАРЛАМЕНТА
²⁰¹⁸
ГЕРМАНИЯ ДУХ БАУХАУСА
33 СЛОВА ²⁰¹⁹ РОССИЯ
О ДИЗАЙНЕ
EVERYBODY IN THE
PLACE: РЕЙВ КАК
ЗАБАСТОВКА
PJ HARVEY: A DOG ²⁰¹⁹ ВЕЛИКОБРИТАНИЯ ИРЛАНДИЯ
CALLED MONEY
²⁰¹⁸ США СТУДИЯ 54 ФИЛЬМ ОТКРЫТИЯ

STUDIO 54
98 МИН
МЭТТ ТИРНАУР
США, 2018

ИСТОРИЯ САМОГО
ИЗВЕСТНОГО НОЧНОГО
КЛУБА В МИРЕ, СТАВШЕГО
СИНОНИМОМ ДИСКО,
НАРКОТИКОВ, СВОБОДЫ
И РАЗВРАТА.

BEAT WEEKEND 9—13.10

ФЕСТИВАЛЬ
ДОКУМЕНТАЛЬНОГО
КИНО О МУЗЫКЕ
И НОВОЙ КУЛЬТУРЕ

КАРО ОКТЯБРЬ
НОВЫЙ АРБАТ 24

ДУХ БАУХАУСА ²⁰¹⁸ ГЕРМАНИЯ
²⁰¹⁸ ВЕЛИКОБРИТАНИЯ EVERYBODY IN THE
PLACE: РЕЙВ КАК
ЗАБАСТОВКА
PJ HARVEY: A DOG
CALLED MONEY
RAVING RIOT: ²⁰¹⁹ РОССИЯ ГРУЗИЯ
РЕЙВ У ПАРЛАМЕНТА
БЕРЛИНСКИЙ

18+

BEATWEEKEND.RU

Electric Red Studio, poster for Beat Film Festival using
typeface CoFo Sans, designed by Maria Doreuli, 2020

121

Varia-
tions
Вари-
ации

Bulgarian form

in collaboration with Krista Radoeva,
type designer (Sofia, Bulgaria)

The topic of Cyrillic is very important for the Bulgarian nation, since the Bulgarian Empire is believed to be the cradle of Cyrillic script. Saint Cyril and Methodius are honoured by many people in the country and the Day of Slavonic Alphabet and Culture was made into an official public holiday. For a long time, Bulgaria was sharing the experience of Cyrillic script development with other Slavic countries. However, some historical coincidences have led to an interesting notion, where Bulgarian type has partially evolved into a new alternative form.

Bulgarian form, also called by some designers Bulgarian Cyrillic, bolgaritsa or oval Cyrillic, contains a lot of characters with letterforms close to Latin script. This deviation from the common development course of Cyrillic script began with the conquest of Bulgaria by the Ottoman Empire in the 14th century. While the script in the Russian Empire was gradually evolving towards the printing era, Bulgaria didn't have access to such technologies. Being beneath the yoke of the Ottomans for almost 500 years, all the way till the end of the 19th century, the nation could only rely on its handwriting. Therefore, when Bulgaria proclaimed independence in 1908, their type tradition was much closer to the Latin one in the sense of the use of calligraphic letterforms, especially for lowercase characters [26].

[26] Type specimen with Bulgarian form characters from the book of Tsoncho Voynikov, 1946

АБВГДЕЖЗИЙКЛМНОП
РСТУФХЦЧШЩЪЬЮЯ
абвгдежзийклмно
прстуфхцчшщъьюя

The second wave of Bulgarian form was largely sparked by the Western influence in the first half of the 20th century. A lot of the leading Bulgarian graphic and type designers were getting their education in German universities, such as the Berlin Academy of Arts or Academy of Fine Arts Leipzig, where the influence of the Latin typographic tradition was inevitable. One of the faces of Bulgarian type revolution was the artist and book designer Boris Angelushev, who used a lot of Cyrillic lettering in his works, which naturally included handwritten shapes of the characters. His unique style has set a trend and inspired other Bulgarian designers to popularise Bulgarian version of Cyrillic [1]. His works also had a great influence on the Bulgarian typographer and illustrator Vasil Yonchev. Together with his wife Olga Yoncheva they have conducted a thorough analysis of Cyrillic typographic heritage, and systematised the key elements and aesthetics of Bulgarian type form. His position as a professor of the National Academy of Arts Sofia in the 1970s gave him an opportunity to spread the knowledge and educate the following generations of designers.

Currently Bulgarian Cyrillic has a twofold status in the country, both literally and figuratively. Graphic designers are using both Russian and Bulgarian forms of Cyrillic, and already a whole generation of people has grown up with these dual reading habits. It can be explained by the extensive use of Russian print type and a strong political influence during the Soviet times, and the lack of modern fonts with Bulgarian glyph sets. There is, however, a group of design activists that advocate for the popularisation and consolidation of Bulgarian form as a part of a national identity. When Bulgaria was entering the European Union in 2007, there was an attempt to constitute Bulgarian forms into a separate Unicode, which fell through. In 2014 a group of type and graphic designers have created an initiative "For Bulgarian Cyrillic", within the framework of which they carry out educational work and try to involve the government in the standardisation of the script [2].

So, what specifically differs Bulgarian script from other versions of Cyrillic? The main philosophy behind it is that lowercase characters should be different from uppercase. Bulgarian Cyrillic is more based on the handwritten forms of certain characters, especially those, that have ascenders and descenders. This makes the text look more dynamic, therefore more legible for the reader. Generally, they are sharing the same concept of natural script development with Latin type.

In Russian Cyrillic only 6 lowercase characters have different letterforms from uppercase, while in Bulgarian it's 22. Bulgarian also has the highest number of characters containing ovals and curved elements compared to Latin and Russian Cyrillic. It is also typical for Bulgarian form to have one-sided serifs on top of the characters. Decorative features are not written in stone and may vary depending on the style of the typeface. However the most important Bulgarian letterforms have already been developed and polished for decades.

[1] "Krassen Krestev: Bulgarian Cyrillic, identity in progress", Aleksandra Samulenkova, Typotalks, May 25, 2015

[2] Initiative "За българска кирилица", cyrillic.bg

А Б В Г Д Е Ё Ж
З И Й К Л М Н О
П Р С Т У Ф Х Ц Ч
Ш Щ Ъ Ы Ь Э Ю Я
а б в г д е ё ж з
и й к л м н о п р
с т у ф х ц ч ш
щ ъ ы ь э ю я

А Б В Г Д Е Ж
З И Й К Л М Н О
П Р С Т У Ф Х Ц Ч
Ш Щ Ъ Ы Ь Э Ю Я
а б в г д е ж з
и й к л м н о п р
с т у ф х ц ч ш
щ ъ ь ю я

[27] Letterform differences in Russian and Bulgarian alphabets

The differences are not that significant when it comes to uppercase characters. There are only three uppercase characters with alternative letterform: Ф, Л and Д. In Russian Cyrillic the oval of Ф is made smaller than О in order to fit the same capital height, while in Bulgarian the oval is made the same size as О, and the stroke is ascending and descending the capital height. As for Л and Д, it is more common in modern Russian typefaces to design them rectangularly, while in Bulgarian Л is designed triangular, and Д can have both shapes. There are also small nuances in letters И and Й, especially in serif typefaces. In the Bulgarian version, the diagonal is connected to the verticals at the top and bottom, which exempts from using two inner strokes that are often found in the Russian version of the letters [27].

Most of the Bulgarian lowercase characters clearly follow the logic of Latin script. As much as 13 Bulgarian lowercase letters are identical to Latin: a g e u ŭ k o n p c m y x. The others either follow the calligraphic path or use ascenders and descenders for the contrast. An interesting detail is that the use of Latin letter m instead of Russian т makes Bulgarian texts 3,5-4% longer, since it's one of the most common characters in Slavic languages. This might be one of the reasons why publishers prefer the Russian Cyrillic in order to save space.

[28] Text set in Russian and Bulgarian forms

Старобългарската азбука, наречена от историка Георги Бакалов Климентовица е първата кирилица, създадена в края на IX век за нуждите на християнизацията на населението на българската държава и Българската църква

Старобългарската азбука, наречена от историка Георги Бакалов Климентовица е първата кирилица, създадена в края на IX век за нуждите на християнизацията на населението на българската държава и Българската църква

Currently the attitude towards Bulgarian form is quite mixed in the design community. Some designers consider it an unnecessary alteration of the script and even perceive it as more of a political move. Others gladly accept it as a revolutionised form of Cyrillic and incorporate it in their design practice. It has also been gaining more and more recognition due to the fact that the fonts with Bulgarian sets are not only created by Bulgarian type designers anymore, but also by internationally acclaimed typographers like Lucas de Groot, Peter Bilak, Ilya Ruderman and others. For the regular font users, however, the lack of fonts with Bulgarian form still remains a problem. The system is not embedded in the computer software used by most of the people, leaving them to the single choice of Russian letterforms.

Whatever the attitude, it's still important to remember that script is a significant part of cultural identity, and the urge to stick to the traditions of your country should be respected. Needless to say, Cyrillic script is still evolving, and the shift from artificial formation to a more natural one might not hurt.

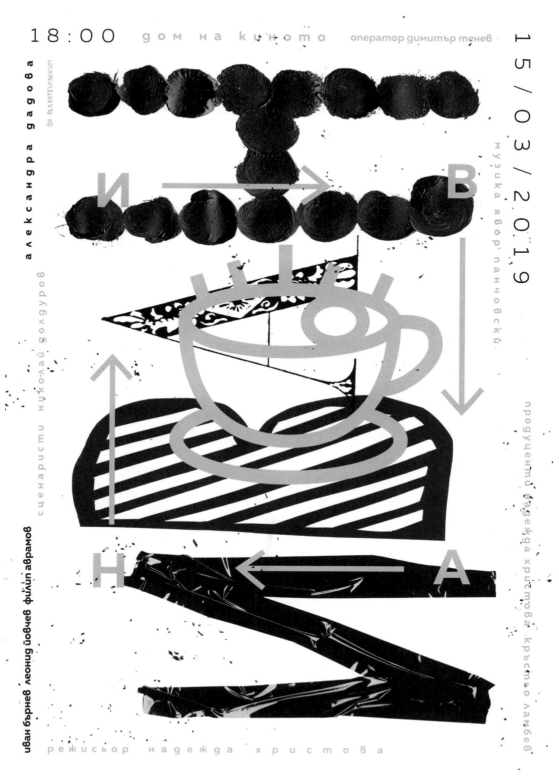

15 / 03 / 2019

александра дадова
фа PLAKTECHNIKUM

музика явор панчовски

продуцентi Надежда христова крьстьо ламбев

сценаристi николай долдуров

иван бърнев леонид йовчев филип абрамов

режисьор надежда христова

Atanas Giew, poster for a short movie "Ivan", 2019

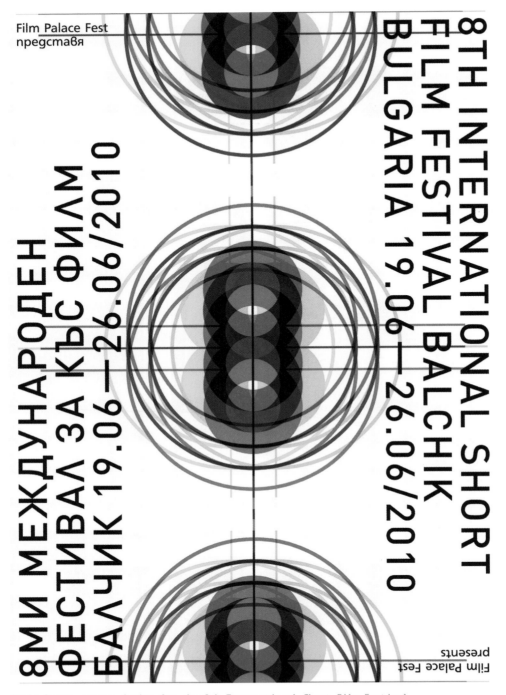

Film Palace Fest
представя

8TH INTERNATIONAL SHORT
FILM FESTIVAL BALCHIK
BULGARIA 19.06—26.06/2010

8МИ МЕЖДУНАРОДЕН
ФЕСТИВАЛ ЗА КЪС ФИЛМ
БАЛЧИК 19.06—26.06/2010

Film Palace Fest
presents

Boris Bonev, poster design for the 8th International Short Film Festival
in Balchik, Bulgaria, 2010

miguel anønimo, booklet
for traveling series
«The Sofia Issue», 2018

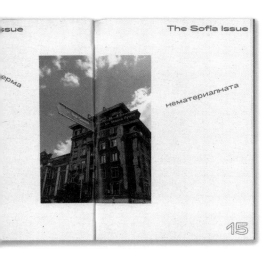

Boris Bonev, cover design for a book
by Jacques Attali «La Crise, et après», 2008

Paul Voggenreiter, portfolio for Plovdiv
based artist Dimitar Shopov, 2021

Paul Voggenreiter, Visual identity for the first edition
of Sofia Art Projects «Intimacy and spectacle in the age of social media», 2021

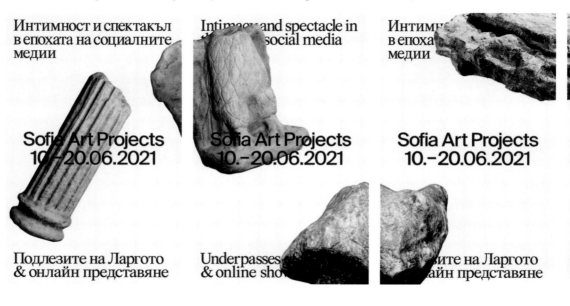

Sofia Art Projects

Intimacy and spectacle in the age of social media

Интимност и спектакъл в епохата на социалните медии

Are there really borders between art and life we would like to keep? The project "Intimacy and Spectacle in the Time of Social Media" aims to explore those liminal situations, frameworks and platforms where parallel and divergent representations of art and the public sphere are possible.

Наистина има ли граници между изкуството и живота, които бихме искали да запазим? Проектът "Интимност и спектакъл в епохата на социалните медии" изследва онези гранични ситуации, рамки и платформи, където са възможни паралелни и размиващи се представяния на изкуството и общест-вената сфера.

Krasimira Butseva, Pauline Boudry & Renate Lorenz, Anetta Mona Chisa & Lucia Tkacova, Lazar Lyutakov, Ivan Moudov, Viktor Ruban, Tracey Snelling, Sasho Stoitsov, Stela Vasileva

curated by Dessislava Dimova, Vessela Nozharova and Vera Mlechevska

Her Accurate Private Mind - a curated streaming program with art videos and live performances.

www.sofiaartprojects.com

Underpasses of the Largo & online showcases

Подлезите на Ларгото & онлайн представяне

10.–20.06.2021

Paul Voggenreiter, Visual identity for the first edition of Sofia Art Projects «Intimacy and spectacle in the age of social media», 2021

Serbian azbuka

in collaboration with Jovana Jocić,
type designer (Belgrade, Serbia)

Serbian Cyrillic is another interesting case worth exploring since this is an alphabet that took on a somewhat alternative path from the more common Russian Cyrillic. The type reform of Peter the Great has had an enormous influence on the development of Cyrillic letterforms throughout all Slavic countries. Most of them have adopted the new graphemes and use them in the modernised form till today. Serbia, however, had its own separate script reform in the 19th century.

Cyrillic has first spread through Serbian principalities in the 11–12th century, when the country was under Bulgarian rule. Therefore the development of the script was quite similar to other Slavic countries, going through the same stages of evolution. Until the reforms of Peter the Great in the 18th century Serbia had used Church Slavonic literary language and old style Cyrillic script. Then, for the next century the Russian influence on the alphabet and letterforms became very visible in both handwritten and printed materials [1]. However in the 19th century philologists started paying more attention to the fact that Russian Cyrillic rules don't fully fit the Serbian language and pronunciation.

First, Serbian philologist and monk Sava Mrkalj has formulated the main principle of the reform: write as you speak. He has revised the Russian Church Cyrillic alphabet, got rid of the unnecessary letters and added several new characters that were important for Serbian phonetics. His other big plan was to introduce vernacular as literary language, which was very much opposed by the church, claiming that Mrkalj is ruining Serbian traditions [2]. His progress was taken over by the linguist Vuk Karadžić, who finalised the alphabet in 1818. However, their revolutionary ideas were officially adopted only in 1868, four years after Karadžić's death.

The Serbian alphabet reform resulted in retaining twenty-four Slavic characters, adding one Latin character Jj and five completely new ones Љљ Њњ Ћћ Ђђ Џџ, which were the combination of liga-

[1] "Short History of the Cyrillic Alphabet", Ivan G. Iliev, International Journal of Russian Studies, Issue No.2, January 2013

[2] "Sava Mrkalj – reforma ćirilice", Adriana Micić, Portal Mladi, December 25, 2015

tures and adopted graphemes from old Romanian and Glagolitic [29]. This gives Serbian typography a more exotic and westernised look compared to Russian form. Currently Serbian Cyrillic is officially used in Serbia, Montenegro and Bosnia and Herzegovina. It has also laid the foundation for the creation of the Macedonian alphabet.

Аа Бб Вв Гг Дд Ђђ Ее Жж Зз
Ии Јј Кк Лл Љљ Мм Нн Њњ Оо
Пп Рр Сс Тт Ћћ Уу Фф Хх Цц
Чч Џџ Шш

Serbian historical handwriting tradition has also made adjustments to some of the italic characters. Lowercase italic letters г, д, п and т have drastically different letterforms, which strongly influences the appearance of the text [30]. However, this is where the main challenge for Serbian Cyrillic appears. The domination of Russian forms, the absence of Serbian alternatives in the Unicode and the lack of typefaces with Serbian stylistic sets seems to be leading to the gradual extinction of the script.

$g\bar{\imath}$ ∂g $n\bar{u}$ $m\bar{u}$

[30] Russian and alternative Serbian italic letterforms of some characters

Although on the state level Cyrillic is the official script of the country, according to the latest surveys the majority of citizens use Latin instead of Cyrillic. This cruel fate has been following the script for centuries, with the Austro-Hungarian Empire forbidding Serbs to use it during the World War I, and later in 1954 with the signing of the Novi Sad Literary Agreement, which made both Latin and Cyrillic alphabets equally acceptable in the countries of former Yugoslavia. Despite its current official status, still not enough educational and preservation work is done in order to popularise the script, which in the future may result in Cyrillic becoming an archaic alphabet in Serbia [3]. This can already be seen in the diminishing number of design projects with Serbian Cyrillic.

The case of Serbian azbuka is an example of the negative effects of globalisation. Ideally the outcome of the global cultural exchange should result in a shared knowledge with which people asso-

3 "Ivan Klajn: Ćirilica će postati arhaično pismo", K. Živanović, Danas, December 15, 2014

134

ciate their collective cultural identities, instead of one culture taking over the other. Education about foreign cultural aspects is supposed to enrich people's world view and help to fight stereotypes and misconceptions about others, which is also the goal of this book in particular. Once again, it's important to remember that script systems are not made-up collections of characters. Cyrillic, as any other existing script, was invented and developed according to the needs of the languages that use it. However, the understanding of the value and the initiative to promote and protect one's heritage should come first and foremost from the carriers of the culture. Or else it has every chance of becoming extinct or devoured by other stronger influences.

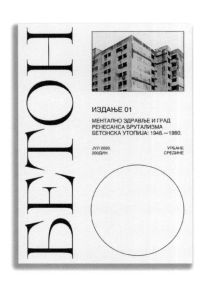

Katarina Escobar Dobrijević, design for concept magazine "Beton", 2020

Jasmina Zornic, typographic experimentation with the word "love" in different languages, 2021

Peter Bankov, poster for the student competition "Identity Crisis"
(Macedonian Cyrillic), 2016

04. X— 31. XII 2019

MOДΕRЛА MODERЛА

ИЗБОР
РАДОВА
ИЗ
КОЛЕКЦИЈЕ
КУЋЕ
ЛЕГАТА

ЛЕГАТ
ПЕТРА ЛУБАРДЕ
ИЛИЧИЋЕВА 1

SELECTION
OF
WORK
FROM
THE
HERITAGE
HOUSE

LEGAT
PETRA LUBARDE
ILIČIĆEVA 1

www.kucalegata.org

Korak Studio, "Moderna" exhibition design and identity
for the Heritage House in Belgrade, 2019

Miloš Ćirić, bilingual wordmark
for the "Besede" theater, 1975

Korak Studio, design of the
October issue of "Bosanska
Vila" magazine, 2019

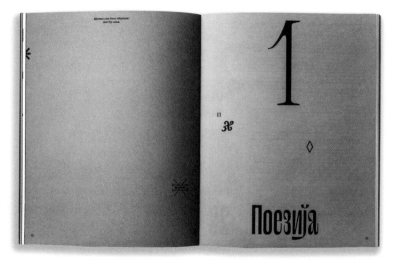

Epilogue

Эпилог

What's next?

The scale and the tempo at which globalisation takes over the world considerably influences all professional areas, and design which functions at the forefront of every culture is not an exception. The tendency for multi-scriptualism is almost an unavoidable perspective. Already big corporations, IT-companies, and cultural organisations are acting on such international levels that require the knowledge of each market's cultural specifics. For a graphic designer in particular this means the knowledge of script, rules of typography, choice of typefaces, colours, visual materials and messages.

These days more and more designers are introduced to multi-scriptual and multicultural projects and experience the challenges related to them. While type designers are given more access to studying foreign scripts through educational institutions, this opportunity is still unavailable for most graphic design students. Especially in countries dominated by Latin script. Therefore, it is important to spread the knowledge here and now.

Besides, human progress was always built on the exchange of knowledge, traditions and experiences. A mix of different influences might produce tremendously interesting and innovative outcomes, in the area of graphic and type design included. So far, we have mostly observed the traditions of Latin type impacting other script systems. Nevertheless, the same way foreign scripts can be a great source of inspiration for Latin type designers, while different ethnic peculiarities might enrich every graphic designer's practice.

Such urge for experimentation and the search for new forms started a long time ago with the development of the so-called "ethnic typefaces" [1]. However, instead of pretending to look foreign and occasionally offending people of other cultures, designers these days can try to make more educated decisions and smarter moves when it comes to multi-scriptual assignments.

At the current stage of development, Cyrillic script still allows a lot of experimentation with shapes, and definitely has tricks to offer to the Latin type. Although the classic forms of many characters are considered to be set, but, as type designer Maria Doreuli said: "Many

[1] Typefaces that represent the Latin alphabet and imitate another writing systems, for example, Arabic, Chinese (chop-suey fonts), Greek, Hebrew and others. Date back to the 19th century

141

signs of good and bad Cyrillic typefaces in reality turn out to be very subjective." This statement allows a certain freedom, which Latin type doesn't always have. Eastern European culture has a lot of historic baggage that slowly but surely comes back to the surface after almost a century of obliteration, and already serves as an inspiration for creatives around the world.

Soyuz Grotesk

designed by
Roman Gornitsky
Leipzig, Germany

distributed by
The Temporary State

One of the earlier examples of experimental type design that involves mutual Cyrillic-Latin influence stems from Soviet times, when in 1963 two Moscow Print Institute students Maxim Zhukov and Yuri Kurbatov created a bootleg Cyrillic version of the modernist typeface "Helvetica", then known as "Neue Haas Grotesk" [31].

АБВГДЕЖЗИ
абвгдежзийкл
ЙКЛМНОПРСТУ
мнопрстуфхич
ФХЦЧШЩЪЫ
шщъыьэюя
ьэюя

[31] Type specimen of "Sowjetische Haas Grotesk", designed by Maxim Zhukov and Yuri Kurbatov, 1963

Young designers, inspired by the German and Swiss modernist type culture were looking for fresh and contemporary solutions in a time when Western products in the USSR were considered a sign of bourgeoisie and were completely unacceptable in the industry [2]. Because of such harsh restrictions, there was no chance for foreign type foundries to legally distribute their typefaces in Soviet countries. Therefore, there was no other choice than to design pirate versions of world-famous fonts.

[2] "Towards an open layout: A letter to Volodya Yefimov", Maxim Zhukov, Type Journal, February 23, 2014

Although inspired by a very clear and structured typeface, "Sowjetische Haas Grotesk" turned out to be much more expressive and radical than its original. This is an example of how an unprejudiced, even partially naive view of a designer can result in something innovative. Zhukov and Kurbatov took the very few expressive elements of "Helvetica" and implemented them all over their new Cyrillic letterforms, creating lots of curvy and rounded shapes. The fact that they also used mostly cursive forms of the characters instead of roman made the typeface look even more unusual. The cherry on top was the very thin strokes used in letters й, ц, щ instead of descenders – the element that doesn't appear in original Linotype design.

The typeface became extremely popular in the design community despite that it was never made into a printing font and only existed on plastic film for photo composition. For years "Sowjetische Haas Grotesk" was used in a logo for one of the most important Soviet design-focused periodicals "Technical Aesthetics". However by the late 80s it was left behind due to the emergence of new Helvetica-like fonts. Until in 2017 Russian type designer Roman Gornitsky rediscovered and digitalised it into "Soyuz Grotesk" typeface.

Gornitsky's main challenge was the creation of the Latin set for the typeface, since following the structure of the original "Helvetica" after such a majestic transformation was out of the question. In order to maintain the modernist spirit and charm of the Cyrillic part, designer reduced the number of ascenders and descenders in Latin characters and kept all the characters only in lowercase style. Other peculiar adjustments involve lowercase r as a mirrored ч, and Bulgarian form for both з and z [3].

[3] "Soyuz Grotesk", Roman Gornitsky, Letters from The Temporary State, October 19, 2017

[32] Latin and Cyrillic samples of "Soyuz Grotesk"

Helvetica
in the eyes of the
soviet type designer

гельветика
глазами советского
шрифтового дизайнера

This mind-blowing case of Latin influencing Cyrillic and back again is only the first in line of demonstrating how a bidirectional approach in typography and type design can breathe new life into conservative script traditions. We as creatives are actually quite lucky to be living in times where access to information about other cultures became so easy. There is a never-ending field of inspiration laying ahead of us.

CSTM Xprmntl 03

designed by
Yury Ostromentsky
Moscow, Russia

distributed by
tomorrow.type.today

The "not so original" idea behind this typeface, according to designer Yury Ostromentsky, lies in constructing the variable font with two very distinct historic styles on both ends and observing what happens right in the middle, at the point of their interpolation. The idea might not be the most original in the world, however the results turned out to be fascinating.

First of all, taking such historically and graphically opposite calligraphic styles like Blackletter and old-style Cyrillic has set the experiment to a good start. Second, not planning and being open minded to whatever comes in the end has led to a fresh and innovative interpretation of classic letterforms. The project has also given the author an opportunity to incorporate Cyrillic in Blackletter style and redesign Latin in ancient Slavic manner.

[33] Blackletter,
Cyrillic and
Medium styles of
CSTM Xprmntl 03

The Blackletter
И кириллица, конечно же

Oldstyle Cyrillic
И кириллица, конечно же

Freaky medium
И кириллица, конечно же

As anything new and undone before, the process turned out to be quite complex and long-lasting. Letters a, k, y, x turned out to be the most challenging, since they have very different forms in both scripts. According to Ostromentsky, the variability of the font also required some animation and directorial skills, since the font had to look legible at any point of interpolation. On the other hand, this particular technology is exactly what currently allows to get revolutionary outcomes in the area of type design. In perspective, variable fonts give us the opportunity to unify any existing styles and scripts, which can result in even more collaborations with Cyrillic in particular.

All in all, this somewhat punkish project is a great example of how revisiting the past and drawing inspiration from other cultures can give life to new forms even in such conservative area as script. As for further experimentation with historic Cyrillic forms, Yury Ostromentsky is not stopping there. In his next project he is planning to create a contemporary version of old-style Cyrillic typeface, as if Petrine type reform has never happened. With exploring which turn Cyrillic script could have taken and incorporating Latin characters into the system, the author is hoping to expand the geography and areas of use of classic old Slavic forms.

Norbert

designed by
Philipp Neumeyer
Berlin, Germany

distributed by
TypeMates

Unfortunately, there are still very few Western designers who take on the risk of designing Cyrillic typefaces. And even fewer of them are brave enough to experiment with it, due to many factors, such as the lack of information on the topic and a common opinion in the community that Cyrillic should be only designed by native users. German type designer Philipp Neumeyer is a rare bird with a sincere interest in Slavic letterforms and a bold attitude towards working with them. He has already designed several typefaces with Cyrillic families that are highly praised by the Russian type design community.

Despite not having any course on Cyrillic script during his education, Phillip has always been fascinated by the mysteriousness of the bulky letters and associations that came from stereotypical movies about criminality, bad guys, and corruption in Russia. By drawing inspiration from his trips to Moscow and Saint Petersburg and consulting Cyrillic type design specialists, he started experimenting on his own fonts that can all be characterised by nonconformity of shapes and ironic mood.

"Norbert is a little bit of everything I've collected over the years. Like old specimens of grotesque typefaces, the photos that I've taken and blurry memories that I have", comments Philipp. The last bit of in-

145

spiration came during his visit to Saint Petersburg, where he saw the typography on the historic facade of the "Au Pont Rouge" department store, constructed at the beginning of the 20th century. More specifically, it was the squarish G with a tail that set the project in action [34].

The font comes in two widths, Breit and Schmal. Additionally each weight is complimented by Kursiv and Kontra styles. It's designed in the mood of early hot metal type families, where at first sight all the letterforms share the same construction, but each individual style creates such a unique texture, that all of them look like completely separate typefaces. Some of the characters are taken to the beautiful extremes, which makes the typeface both expressive and classy, depending on your design needs.

[35] Norbert Breit

Au Pont Rouge
we will meet again!

У Красного моста
мы встретимся с тобою!

Norbert Schmal

Or at the Garment factory
that was constructed in the 18th century.

Ну, или у Швейной фабрики Володарского,
которую впервые построили еще в восемнадцатом веке.

Some consider the Cyrillic part to be slightly naive and partially wrong. However, the designer's lack of expertise in the topic and his unbiased view of the script is exactly what makes all the letterforms so unique, playful and fresh. And this might be the one approach that will bring both Latin and Cyrillic type to the next level – exploring and taking a fresh look at unfamiliar sources.

KyivType

designed by
Dmitry Rastvortsev
Sumy, Ukraine

distributed
for free

Development of KyivType font was organised as a part of an unofficial Kyiv city identity. It was a free designer initiative launched by three big Ukrainian design studios Projector, Dmytro Bulanov Creative Büro, and Banda Agency in 2019. After designing the logo in the shape of a chestnut leaf that has served as a symbol of Ukraine's capital for decades, it was decided that identity also needs a typeface that could be freely distributed thus popularising the new contemporary image of the city. The work was commissioned to type designer Dmitry Rastvortsev, who has previously worked on several other projects involving city identities and the development of historic Ukrainian typefaces.

The general message behind the typeface is the diversity of Ukraine's capital. An eclectic combination of classical and contemporary architecture, rapid technical development, and underground culture are all represented in the elements of KyivType. This dynamic is also reflected in the variability of the font. The most interesting part is that besides the classic Sans and Serif settings, the designer also developed the Titling style.

Titling style is inspired by the typefaces of Ukrainian modernists, such as Heorhiy Narbut [36] and Vasyl Khomenko. The distinguishing features of their typography are asymmetrical serifs and the use of pre-Petrine letterforms that are graphically closer to their Greek originals. This style was adopted and popularised at the beginning of the 20th century, when Ukraine gained its sovereignty from the Russian Empire for a short period of time and was actively rethinking its cultural identity.

[36] A fragment from the cover of "Mystetstvo" magazine, designed by Heorhiy Narbut, 1919

МИСТЕЦТВО

Літературно-мистецький тижневик відділ мистецтв при

НАРКОМПРОСІ

Just like Bulgarian form, these stylistic features have slowly but surely developed into a recognisable tradition of Ukrainian typography and are often cited by Ukrainian type designers in order to achieve an authentic image. One can notice that the use of some Greek letters, like N, Z, Σ and a bigger amount of ascending and descending elements makes Ukrainian text look graphically closer to Latin. And last but not the least, this is another great example of foreign traditions influencing the look of the Latin part of the font, since naturally it was designed as an addition to the Cyrillic family.

[37] KyivType Sans

Avant-garde
expressive simplicity
ну, звичайно ж, кирилиця

KyivType Serif

Vasyl Khomenko
Ukrainian aesthetics
національна іденпичніспь

KyivType Titling

Heorhiy Narbut
eclectic & diverse
українɕький модерnízм

Just go for it!

If you are holding this book in your hands and have read it all the way to this final chapter, it means that you are definitely interested in the topic of Cyrillic type and have enough basic knowledge to start designing with it. So just go for it! Whatever your motivation is, whether it's to make your design look more exotic, contribute to the diversity, or just practice and educate yourself and others – those are all legit reasons to try working with this peculiar yet beautiful script.

Keep in mind the main theses of this book. Cyrillic is one of the closest scripts to Latin by the origins and graphics. Typographic rules are also quite similar to Latin, however some adjustments in tracking, leading, type size, and attention to details are required. Try to refrain from using Cyrillic characters as substitutes for Latin and double-check your designs with native speakers to avoid the risk of cultural appropriation. Check out Eastern European type designers and foundries. And most importantly, don't listen to those who say that only natives are allowed to work with the script.

Experimentation and open-mindedness have always been the moving force of progress. Because of diverse perspectives and visions, collaboration between designers-users of different scripts can result in new revolutionary approaches towards the future development of type and design. While personally, the knowledge of foreign script systems might enrich every designer's professional experience, result in new, surprising solutions, and increase the variety and quantity of their clientele and target audience.

Not to mention the active ongoing exchange of information due to rapid globalisation, which humans experience today, and the huge impact it's making on all professional practices that deal with communication. The modern world requires the knowledge and serious analysis of cultural characteristics in order to promote a product or convey a message. Therefore, in the Western world in particular designers experience the growing demand towards multilingual design as a mean of intercultural communication. At this point you possess the necessary skills to make a contribution to this process. All that's left is a little bit of practice.

Make sure to check out the list of reading recommendations at the end of this book. Since there are very few printed publications dedicated to this topic (otherwise there would have been no need in working on this book), and even less are published in English, you can take a look at several websites that produce an up-to-date material on the topic of Cyrillic type and graphic design. And last but not least, don't hesitate to reach out to Eastern European designers for any support in your future Cyrillic projects. Design community is quite a small family, and now more than ever designers are willing to share and popularise the knowledge about their native scripts.

References
Ссылки

Picture credits

p.13 [2]   "Russian Criminal Tattoo Encyclopaedia Volume I", front cover.
            Designed and published by FUEL, 2004

p.14 [3]   Photo: Courtesy of Yulia Yefimtchuk

p.14 [4]   Photo: Courtesy of Adidas and Gosha Rubchinskiy

p.15 [5]   Photo: Courtesy of Sputnik1985

p.15 [6]   Photo: Courtesy of Heron Preston

p.16 [8]   Illustration from the article
            "Font scandal at FIFA World Cup",
            type.today, July 10, 2018

p.18 [9]   Photo: Courtesy of H&M

p.18 [10]   Photo: Yana Vekshyna

p.37   Photo: Anna Kulachek

p.45 [11]   Codex Tischendorfianus IV, fragment
            Bodleian Library, National Library of Russia

p.45 [12]   The Kiev Missal, fragment
            V.I. Vernadsky National Library of Ukraine

p.47 [13]   Ostromir Gospels, fragment
            The National Library of Russia

p.47 [14]   The Tale of Bygone Years, Radziwill Chronicle, fragment
            Library of the Russian Academy of Sciences

p.48 [15]   Poluustav samples
            Chekunova, Antonina. Русское Кириллическое
            Письмо XI-XVIII Вв.
            Moscow: RGGU, 2010

p.48 [16]   Illustrated Chronicle of Ivan the Terrible, fragment
            Russian State Historical Museum

p.49 [17]   Romain du Roi, bitmap
             Jacques Jaugeon, Philippe Grandjean

p.50 [18]   Illustration: Vladimir Lobachov
             "On the appearance and development of Cyrillic letterforms",
             Eugene Yukechev, Type Journal, September 21, 2020

p.51 [19]   Aleksandr Rodchenko, fragment from the book cover "Itogo"
             by Sergey Tretyakov. Gosizdat (State Publishing House), 1924
             Courtesy of The Museum of Modern Art. Jan Tschichold Collection,
             Gift of Philip Johnson.

p.52 [20]   Sergei Chekhonin, fragment from the book cover "Gosti"
             by Elizaveta Polonskaya. Publishing Partnership Kniga, 1924
             "Сквозь мглу и хаос", Aleksey Dombrovskiy,
             Type Journal, October 29, 2014

p.52 [21]   Lateinisch medium condensed sample
             "История одного стандарта", Konstantin Golovchenko,
             Type Journal, October 29, 2014

p.62 [23]   Illustration: Yana Vekshyna
             "Layering of type", Ilya Ruderman

p.69 [24]   Illustration: Yana Vekshyna

p.112 [25]   Illustration: Jovana Jocić

p.115   Photo: Kseniya Yamutova

p.123 [26]   Type specimen
             Voynikov, Tsoncho. Образци шрифтове. Sofia, 1946

p.138–139   Miloš Ćirić, wordmark for a theater "Besede", 1975
             Ćirić, M. Graphic identification 1961-1981. Belgrade: Serbian Literary
             Cooperative; Museum of Applied Art, Belgrade

p.142 [31]   Unautorised Cyrillic version of Helvetica, Maxim Zhukov, Yuri Kurbatov
             "Техническая эстетика: эпизоды из жизни легендарного бюллетеня",
             Sergey Petrov, Type Journal, January 24, 2020

p.142 [34]   Photo: Philipp Neumeyer

p.147 [36]   Heorhiy Narbut, fragment from the cover of "Mystetstvo" magazine,
             Kyiv, 1919

154

Quotes

p.14–15   Anastasiia Fedorova. "Word up: How Cyrillic Typography Became the Lingua Franca for Underground Fashion", The Calvert Journal, June 6, 2014.

p.42-43   Gerry Leonidas, Alexei Vanyashin, Eugene Yukechev. "Gerry Leonidas on teaching typeface design", Type Journal, March 27, 2014.

p.66-67   Peter Bankov in Bi-Scriptual: Typography and Graphic Design with Multiple Script Systems. Wittner, Sascha Thoma, Timm Hartmann (eds.) Salenstein: Niggli, 2019, p.74

p.72-73   Yuri Gordon. Книга про буквы от А до Я. Moscow: Izdat. Studii Artemija Lebedeva, 2006, p.10

Further reading

Wittner, Ben; Sascha Thoma and Hartmann, Timm. *Bi-Scriptual: Typography and Graphic Design with Multiple Script Systems.* Salenstein: Niggli, 2019

Gabbasov, Rustam and Eugene Yukechev. *Cyrillic Type Travel Book Commented.* Moscow: Schrift Publishers, 2019

Hakala, Hanna. *Notes on the Design of DTL Valiance Cyrillic.* Hertogenbosch: Dutch Type Library, 2013

Dowling, Jon and Céline Leterme. *From Eastern Europe.* West Sussex: Counter-Print, 2018

Gordon, Yuri. *Книга про буквы от А до Я.* Moscow: Izdat. Studii Artemija Lebedeva, 2006

Krichevskiy, Vladimir and Aleksey Dombrovskiy. *Два Шрифта Одной Революции.* Moscow: Masterskaia, 2014

Chekunova, Antonina. *Русское Кириллическое Письмо XI-XVIII Вв.* Moscow: RGGU, 2010

type.today/en
Type.today – a collection of high-quality typefaces with Cyrillic families and online journal with relevant articles and interviews from the field of design.

typejournal.ru/en
Type Journal – an online journal devoted to type design, visual culture and typography in the Russian-speaking world.

tipometar.org
Tipometar – a collection of articles about Serbian type design and history.

cyreading.blogspot.com
Cyrillic Readings (in Ukrainian) – articles and samples of Ukrainian and Estern European graphic design.

Imprint

Author, design	Yana Vekshyna
Editing	Seth Tripp
Proofreading	Friederike Christoph Sandra Ellegiers
Experts	Maria Doreuli Anna Kulachek Krista Radoeva Jovana Jocić
Special thanks	Ben Wittner and studio Eps51 Ivan Babenko Alexander Tibus Claudia Baumann Sharmila Sandrasegar Kyrylo Tkachov
Typefaces	Grafier (PangramPangram) Neue Haas Unica (Monotype) PT Mono (Paratype) Spectral (Production Type) Kazimir (CSTM Fonts) Permian (Art. Lebedev Studio) Vollkorn (Friedrich Althausen)
Paper	Pergraphica Natural Rough 120 g/m²
Prototype	Bachelor Thesis project at Berlin International University of Applied Sciences, BA Graphic Design and Visual Communication, class of 2020. Supervisors: Prof. Alexander Tibus, Benjamin Wittner (Eps51)
With support of	**berlin international** UNIVERSITY OF APPLIED SCIENCES

The Deutsche Nationalbibliothek lists this publication in the Deutsche Nationalbibliografie; detailed bibliographic data are available on the Internet at http://dnb.dnb.de

ISBN 978-3-7212-1018-7

© 2023 Niggli, imprint of Braun Publishing AG, Salenstein
www.niggli.ch

1st edition 2023

Yana Vekshyna is a graphic designer and illustrator living and working in Berlin. Born in Kyiv, Ukraine, she has moved to Germany to receive design education, and graduated from Berlin International University of Applied Sciences with a Bachelor degree in Graphic Design and Visual Communication. Coming from a mixed national and educational background, Yana's main points of interest are multi-cultural editorial, print and digital design and multi-scriptual typography.

Krista Radoeva is a designer with a focus on typography and type design. Born in Bulgaria, she grew up with a love for history and language and continued exploring these subjects in her work as a graphic design student at Central Saint Martins College of Art and Design in London. Her studies and her work experience in publication design both in the UK and Bulgaria influenced her to pursue further education in type design on the Type and Media course in The Hague. Underlining themes in her work relationships between language, history, typography and experimentation. During her time in The Hague, alongside working on her final project, she had the opportunity to pursue her interest in Cyrillic type design.

Jovana Jocić is a type designer & lettering artist from Belgrade, Serbia. After receiving a MA in Type Design at the University of Arts in Belgrade, she graduated from the Type and Media course. Currently Jovana is working as a freelance type designer focusing on Latin and Cyrillic scripts, and providing consultations on Cyrillic. Born and raised in Eastern Europe, Jovana aspires to raise awareness and public knowledge of non-Latin scripts and their role in contemporary design.